ASSEMBLIES from the GALLERY

A complete resource for
collective worship using paintings
from the National Gallery, London

MARGARET COOLING

RELIGIOUS AND MORAL EDUCATION PRESS

PUBLISHED BY RMEP IN ASSOCIATION WITH NATIONAL GALLERY COMPANY LIMITED AND THE STAPLEFORD CENTRE

Published by Religious and Moral Education Press
A division of SCM-Canterbury Press Ltd
A wholly owned subsidiary of Hymns Ancient & Modern Ltd
St Mary's Works, St Mary's Plain
Norwich, Norfolk NR3 3BH

First published 2000

New edition with CD-ROM first published 2006

ISBN 978 1 85175 335 2

This book and CD-ROM have been developed as a joint venture by Religious and Moral Education Press, National Gallery Company Limited and the Stapleford Centre.

 THE STAPLEFORD CENTRE

The Stapleford Centre, The Old Lace Mill, Frederick Road, Stapleford, Nottingham NG9 8NF

Tel: 0115 939 6270
Fax: 0115 939 2076

e-mail: admin@stapleford-centre.org
Website: www.stapleford-centre.org

Acknowledgements

I would like to express my gratitude to the following people for help with this manuscript: Erika Langmuir, Elaine Cooke, Jaqui Emery and Diane Walker. I would also like to thank the staff and pupils of the following schools for trialling this material.

Christ the King Roman Catholic Secondary School, Arnold, Nottingham.
Valewood School, Crosby, Merseyside.
Needham Market Middle School, Needham Market, Suffolk.
Gillots Secondary School, Henley, Oxon.
Stevenson Junior School, Stapleford, Nottingham.
St John's Church of England (Voluntary Controlled) School, Stapleford, Nottingham.
George Spencer Secondary School, Stapleford, Nottingham.
Range High School, Formby, Merseyside.
Thornton Primary School, Thornton, Merseyside.
Formby High School, Formby, Merseyside.

The following paintings have been reproduced with the permission of The National Gallery, London:
'A Jesse Tree', attributed to Girolamo Genga
'The Annunciation' by Duccio
'The Adoration of the Shepherds' by Guido Reni
'The Marriage at Cana' by Mattia Preti
'Christ teaching from Saint Peter's Boat on the Lake of Gennesaret' by Herman Saftleven
'Christ addressing a Kneeling Woman' by Paolo Veronese
'Christ blessing the Children' by Nicolaes Maes
'Christ washing his Disciples' Feet' by Jacopo Tintoretto
'The Betrayal of Christ' by Ugolino di Nerio
'Christ carrying his Cross' by Giampietrino
'Christ rising from the Tomb' by Ferrari Gaudenzio
'The Virgin and Child Enthroned' (detail) by Margarito of Arezzo

'The Whether Outlook' and 'Gone and Forgotten' are taken from *Stuff and Nonsense* copyright © 1989 Gordon Bailey. Used with permission of Lion Hudson plc.
'The Apostles' Rap' by Colin Humphreys is © Colin Humphreys and used with permission.
'The Surprise' by Bob Hartman is taken from *Angels, Angels All Around* by Bob Hartman, published by Lion Hudson plc 1995. Copyright © 1993 Bob Hartman.
'The Rights of the Child' is adapted by the author from the UNICEF web site.
'The Waiter' was inspired by a sketch performed by Nigel Forde.

Designed and typeset by TOPICS – The Creative Partnership, Exeter
Illustrations by Jane Taylor
Printed in Great Britain by Brightsea Ltd, Exeter for SCM-Canterbury Press Ltd, Norwich

Contents

Introduction

Art and Christian worship

In the Christian tradition, there has been a long connection between art and worship. From earliest Christian times, paintings decorated catacombs and the walls of house churches. Later, churches were covered in beautiful mosaics and paintings, not as decoration, but as part of worship itself. Icons became an important part of Christian worship and continue to be so in the Orthodox Churches (Greek, Russian, etc.). (Icons are paintings – often of Christ and the saints – on panels.)

There were two short periods (726–780 and 815–842) when art, particularly in the form of icons, came under attack. Some people thought it inappropriate to depict Christ, who Christians believe is divine. However, those who used icons in worship saw them as an assertion that Jesus really did live as a human being, and anyone who is really human can be represented in art. A third, and longer, period of reaction against art occurred in the sixteenth and early seventeenth centuries. Some Protestants feared that art was a distraction in worship. Others thought that it encouraged a form of idolatry and broke the second commandment ('Make no graven image').

Despite these intermittent reactions, various art forms flourished: sculpture, illuminated manuscripts, stained glass, embroidery and painting. Throughout Christendom churches and chapels were embellished with works of art.

The art in churches functions in a variety of ways. It helps to create a sense of otherness and a spiritual dimension which is an essential part of worship. Many paintings seem to shine with light which gives the sense of another world. Art holds sacred characters up to the worshippers' gaze and encourages people to reflect on them. It communicates stories and beliefs and – by its use of colour, symbol and gesture – conveys the meaning and significance of those stories and beliefs. Art stimulates the imagination, emotions and senses so that worship is not just a cerebral affair.

Art and school worship

Schools are very different from churches. Schools are required to provide the *opportunity* for worship. In England the majority of acts of worship (assemblies) are also required to be *wholly or mainly of a broadly Christian character*. At the same time, worship has to be appropriate to the age, aptitude and background of the pupils. The teacher is therefore required to perform a balancing act, giving the pupils the opportunity to worship, without compulsion and without trespassing on their integrity.

Basing assemblies around art may help teachers in this balancing act, for the art acts as a distancing device, without making the material irrelevant or robbing it of its power. Pupils can look at a story through the eyes of the artist. They can explore the artist's ideas, feelings and beliefs about a Christian subject without having to assent to them. Art offers the pupil the opportunity to experience the reverence felt by the artist without necessarily having to share that reverence.

For example, Assembly 24 uses the painting *The Virgin and Child Enthroned* (detail) by Margarito of Arezzo. It also explores the Christian belief of Jesus as both human yet Son of God. The painting helps teachers handle this sensitive subject, for the teacher can point out the way the *artist* has suggested this belief by the way Jesus is clothed as an important adult on a throne yet is drawn as a baby. The artist's imagination/belief acts as a buffer.

Will it interest them?

The introduction of a visual element in assemblies helps to sustain interest, but if pupils are just confronted with these paintings they may feel they are rather old-fashioned art and some pupils will assume that they will not be of interest. They need to see the relevance of the paintings, and the stories on which they are based. For this reason, links with human experience, integral to each painting, have been chosen for the assemblies. Drama, poetry, video and everyday experiences are also included. These assemblies can also be linked to everyday events and to current affairs. For example, Assembly 4 relates to refugees and could be linked to current news items. These connections cannot be made in the text as they will be constantly changing. Teachers are requested to insert references to items in the news, as appropriate.

Looking at the paintings

Details of the paintings are referred to in each assembly. Teachers may also like to give their pupils a time of quiet to reflect on them, thinking about the mood of the painting, its colours and images.

Note: **Christ carrying his cross** (page 36) Some teachers may feel the painting is not appropriate for their school. In that case, teachers should choose activities from the assemblies that do not rely on the painting.

Using this resource

Themes

Each assembly has a religious theme but it is also linked to a related theme in human experience. This allows all pupils to take something from the assembly. The assemblies are arranged in the order of events as they occur in the biblical narrative. Teachers can select from these to create their own themes. The assemblies can be delivered in any order. Individual assemblies can also be used for 'one-off' special occasions.

Pupil participation

There are plenty of opportunities for pupils to participate. Pupils can read the biblical material, point out details in the painting, read poems and take part in drama and other activities. Secondary pupils are often reluctant to take part and for this reason participation is not crucial to the assemblies; alternatives are provided.

The length of the assembly

Schools vary in the time that is allocated to assembly. The assemblies provided can be reduced to suit the time available.

Introduction

Each assembly has an introductory section. This introduces the theme and helps to link the painting and the biblical material with human experience.

Younger pupils/older pupils/ instructions for teachers

The assemblies are aimed at pupils aged 7–14. Material is provided for both age groups. When preparing, teachers should read the *whole* assembly. Where no age group is suggested, the material is meant for all pupils. Some words may need replacing or explaining for younger pupils. Text in italic type usually indicates instructions for teachers.

Core material

The core material usually concerns the painting and often the biblical material. It is in this section that the religious theme is explored in detail.

Something to think about

This section has been provided for those who prefer a time for thought rather than a prayer.

Optional prayer

Teachers can use the prayer if that is appropriate for their situation.

Biblical material

The biblical material has been rephrased to make it easy to read.

Information on the artist

This background information is for teachers. Some teachers may wish to extract details and use them as part of the assembly.

Drama and video options

Suggestions for the use of drama and video are included, but alternatives are also provided for teachers who do not wish to use these options.

Music

Music is suggested for primary schools. The songs selected are Christian in content. Some teachers may wish to substitute more general songs.

Introducing the assemblies

These assemblies are based on works of art which depict incidents from the life of Jesus or Christian beliefs about him. It is important that pupils know this. Assemblies can be introduced in a way that makes this clear to pupils. For example:

'Today we are looking at the story of …. This is a Christian story and comes from the Bible.'

'Today we are going to explore Christian beliefs about Jesus, using a painting.'

Phrases such as 'Christians believe …' should be used. Such phrases allow pupils to decide their stance towards the material. For some, it will be identification (This is my story/belief). For others, it will be understanding (Now I understand why Christians...). Pupils should feel free to respond to the material at any level as long as it is respectful of other people's beliefs. They should not feel that assent is required.

Health and safety

All activities should be conducted with health and safety considerations in mind. Teachers are referred to their health and safety document. When using candles always have damp sand available.

The CD-ROM

Images of the paintings are provided on the CD. These may be projected from the disk or printed onto an acetate for use on an overhead projector by the purchaser or the purchaser's school/organization only.

The CD contains additional items needed to deliver the assemblies and some optional items such as drama scripts. This material may all be printed. Where required, enlarged copies may be made on the photocopier or these items may be projected from the disk.

Material on the CD is indicated by the symbol O. For a full CD index, see pages 46–48.

A Jesse Tree

attributed to Girolamo Genga (1476–1547)

Background to the painting

Date: 16th century

Medium: gum or egg white? on parchment or paper

Dimensions: 22.2 cm x 14 cm

Mary, with Jesus upon her lap, can be seen at the top of the Jesse tree. Jesse, the father of King David, sleeps below. On the branches of the tree can be seen Jesus' ancestors. It was thought that Giulio Clovio (1498–1578), the leading illuminator of the sixteenth century in Italy, was the artist who painted this Jesse tree. It is now thought to be closer to the style of Girolamo Genga. *(Jee-rroh-lah-mo Jeng-a).* Genga worked chiefly in his native town of Urbino, but also worked in Florence, Siena, Rome and Mantua. Although he worked mainly as a painter, later in life he restored and designed houses and churches. Genga may also have designed theatre sets.

Biblical material

Matthew 1:6–16 (extract)

This is a list of the ancestors of Jesus Christ ...

Jesse was the father of King David
David was the father of Solomon
Solomon was the father of Rehoboam
Rehoboam was the father of Abijah
Abijah was the father of Asa
Asa was the father of Jehoshaphat
Jehoshaphat was the father of Jehoram
Jehoram was the father of Uzziah
Uzziah was the father of Jotham
Jotham was the father of Ahaz
Ahaz was the father of Hezekiah
Hezekiah was the father of Manasseh
Manasseh was the father of Amon
Amon was the father of Josiah
Josiah was the father of Jeconiah
Jeconiah was the father of Shealtiel
Shealtiel was the father of Zerubbabel
Zerubbabel was the father of Abiud
Abiud was the father of Eliakim
Eliakim was the father of Azor
Azor was the father of Zadok

Zadok was the father of Akim
Akim was the father of Eliud
Eliud was the father of Eleazar
Eleazar was the father of Matthan
Matthan was the father of Jacob
Jacob was the father of Joseph
who was the husband of Mary.
Mary was the mother of Jesus.

(This can be read in relay, each pupil taking one line and holding a card with the name that occurs at the beginning of the line. Don't worry if it sounds like a boring list – that is the point!)

Note: Jesus' ancestors are traced through Joseph, who was not Jesus' biological father according to Christian belief. This follows the custom of the day. Legal fatherhood was important and this genealogy gave Jesus the status of eldest son of Joseph. We are not told about Mary's ancestors. She, too, could have been a descendant of David.

Assembly 1

Themes: People are more than names or numbers/Jesus, a real person

 Painting: A Jesse Tree
attributed to Girolamo Genga

You will need:
- Enlarged copies of the identity cards [**O** S1a, b, c] (or use **O** S1c only, covering the photograph and name with your hand when required)
- Either an enlarged copy of the family tree [**O** S1d/2a] or your own drawing
- Image of **A Jesse Tree** [**O** P1/2]

Introduction

We all have different numbers. You have a medical number. If you have ever been to hospital you will have a hospital number. As you grow older you collect various numbers, such as credit card numbers, bank account numbers and so on. By the time you are 18 you might look like this.

Write these up for all to see:
Hospital number: D45545
Bank account number: 475698
National Insurance number: TS 77 65 21 E

Younger pupils
Labels bearing the different numbers can be attached to a pupil.

Sometimes people carry identity cards, they too include a number. *Show the copy of the card without the photograph and the name.* If we reduce people to numbers we know little about them. Is the person who is hospital number D45545 male or female, tall or short, likeable or bad tempered? *Ask pupils to guess.*

If we add a name it is slightly more helpful. *Show the identity card with name and number.* What does this tell us about the person? Even names only take us so far. There might be more than one Aaron Smith. (If appropriate, use examples from your school of two pupils with the same name.) We still know little about the person. *Read the biblical material.*

Younger pupils
Choose just a few names from the list of Jesus' ancestors to read from the biblical material.

Older pupils
Use all of the biblical material.

We know almost nothing about many of the people on Jesus' family tree: it just reads like a boring list of names. If we had pictures of some of these people it might help. *Show the identity card with photograph and explain how this makes it seem more like information about a real person.* What does the picture tell us about Aaron? We are going to look at how one artist coped with the same problem – how to make someone seem like a real person rather than just a number or a name.

Core material

Show the painting. Explain what a family tree is and use either the family tree provided or your own drawing. Explain that the word 'tree' is used as a word picture and the artist is turning the word picture into a painting. If the pupils look closely they will see a tree trunk winding up the centre of the painting with branches on either side. Each of the branches contains a picture.

The artist, Girolamo Genga, has drawn people on Jesus' family tree, which makes them feel more real. By doing this he impresses on the viewer that, for him, as for Christians, Jesus was a real person with real grandparents and great-grandparents. Jesus sits at the top of the tree on Mary's lap. His relations (ancestors) can be seen on the branches. They wear crowns, so we know that many of them were kings. At the bottom of the picture sleeps Jesse, the father of King David, one of Jesus' ancestors.

When Genga painted Jesus' family tree he placed faces on it. This stopped Jesus being just a name or a number on a list. He was not child number 453200. Neither was he just Jesus – a common name at the time that Jesus was born. He was Jesus son of Mary, descendant (great-great- ... grandson of Jesse). This was the artist's way of conveying the Christian belief that Jesus was a real person, who lived in Israel and who was probably born between 4 and 6 B.C.E.

Something to think about

It is very easy to reduce people to numbers or names. Names and numbers can be treated as if they don't matter. Real people do matter.

Optional prayer

To some, I *(ask pupils silently to add their own name if they wish)* am just a number.
To some, I *(ask pupils silently to add their own name if they wish)* am just a name on a list.
To you, I am unique, a person. Thank you, Lord, that my name is written on your hand and is never forgotten.

Music suggestions

'If I were a butterfly', www.butterflysong.com
'From my knees to my nose' and 'God knows my name', *Children's Praise*, compiled by P. Burt et al. (Marshall Pickering, 1991).

Assembly 2

Themes: Famous and ordinary/Jesus' ancestors

Painting: A Jesse Tree
attributed to Girolamo Genga

You will need:
- Enlarged copy of the family tree [O S1d/2a]
- Family tree information [O S2b]
- Image of **A Jesse Tree** [O P1/2]

Introduction

Today we are going to look at family trees. *Show the family tree. Read the descriptions of each person.* Families are often made up of a mixture of people – famous and ordinary. Jesus' family tree also has famous and ordinary people on it.

> **Younger pupils**
> *Explain that the word 'tree' is used as a word picture (the lines can look like branches).*

Core material

Show the painting. This painting, by Girolamo Genga, depicts the family tree of Jesus. As you see, it is painted literally as a tree. The tree winds up the centre of the panel from a sleeping Jesse who was the father of King David. The artist has painted it this way because his painting is based on a passage from the Bible. In the Bible (Isaiah 11:1–4) it says that:

A shoot will spring up from the stump of Jesse ... God's Spirit will be on him. He will be wise and understanding. He will be full of knowledge and power ... He will not judge others just by what he sees, neither will he make decisions just on what he hears; he will judge people with fairness and justice.

This does not mean that Jesse was literally a tree stump and grew branches as the artist has shown! The artist was simply making the word picture (Jesse's family tree) visual. The verse from the Bible means that one of Jesse's descendants (children, grandchildren, etc.) will be a special person sent by God. Christians believe that Jesus was that person. That is why the trunk of the tree in the picture starts in Jesse and ends with Jesus, sitting on Mary's lap, on the top branches. We are going to listen to a reading of Jesus' family tree from the Bible.

> **Younger pupils**
> *Choose just a few names to read from the list of Jesus' ancestors in the biblical material, but make sure you include Akim.*
>
> **Older pupils**
> *Use all of the biblical material.*

If the artist, Genga, had tried to paint all of Jesus' family tree it would have been huge, so he selected certain people. In the painting, on either side of Jesus, appear many of his ancestors (grandparents, great-grandparents, etc.), all of them wearing crowns. The artist wanted to communicate the idea that Jesus is a king so he chose many of the kings from the list of Jesus' ancestors given in the Bible. *(Explain that Jesus was not the king of a country; Christians call him 'The King of Love'.)*

The artist has left out many of the people the Bible includes because they do not fit in with his theme of kingship. He included King David, a famous king who most people remember as the one who slew the gigantic warrior Goliath. David had many other talents. He could write poetry, he was a courageous soldier, he was good at music. David was the sort of person you would want on your family tree. He was famous like Aunt Beatrice and brave like Grandfather Reg. *(Refer back to the introduction.)*

But the artist has left out many people from Jesus' family tree. For example, Akim is missing. We know nothing about Akim beside the fact that he was the father of Eliud. Maybe he was ordinary like Great-great-grandfather Frederick. *(Refer back to the introduction.)*

Something to think about

Look at the painting. Genga did not include people like Akim because they did not fit in with his theme of kingship. Jesus' family tree was, however, 'mixed'. There were famous people in it and ordinary ones. We cannot all be famous and we have to be careful about assessing people just on their status or importance. The Bible includes a very full list of Jesus' ancestors: it includes ordinary people such as Akim as well as famous ones such as David. For Christians this is important: it means that Jesus was like other people, he was 'one of us' and had ordinary ancestors as well as famous ones. It also shows the value placed on ordinary people by the gospel writer.

Optional prayer

The poet John Donne said that fame was not something to be sought, neither was it something to be avoided. Help us, God, to handle what life brings us, secure in the knowledge that you do not judge a person on how famous or how ordinary they are, but on what they have done with the talents you gave them.

Music suggestions

'Hark the glad sound' and 'O come, O come, Emmanuel', *Junior Praise 1*, compiled by P. Horrobin and G. Leavers (Marshall Pickering, 1986).

The Annunciation

by Duccio (active 1278; died 1318)

Background to the painting

Date: 1311

Medium: egg (identified) on poplar, painted surface

Dimensions: 43 cm x 44 cm

Duccio *(Doo-choh)* worked mainly in Siena, where he ran a large workshop. He was one of the most important painters of the fourteenth century. This painting was the first scene on the front predella (base) of Duccio's huge altarpiece (5.00 m x 4.68 m) for the Cathedral of Siena. It was installed in the Cathedral in 1311, after being carried in a great procession through the street. Shops were closed for the day and people followed the altarpiece through the streets, bearing lights and ringing bells. The predella contained scenes from the infancy of Jesus. Infra-red imaging shows the drawing under the paint, done with a quill pen, probably by Duccio himself rather than a member of his workshop. There is also an orange area underneath the angel's wing which probably should have been gold but someone forgot to gild it. Mary's book is opened and on the page are the words (in Latin): Behold a Virgin shall conceive and bear a son and he shall be called Emmanuel (Isaiah 7:14). The lilies in a vase symbolize the Virgin's purity. Within a beam of light, the Holy Spirit descends in the form of a dove.

Biblical material

Luke 1:26–38

God sent the angel Gabriel to a small town in Galilee called Nazareth. He sent him with a message to a virgin called Mary who was engaged to be married to a man named Joseph. Joseph belonged to the family of King David.

The angel greeted Mary and said, 'Peace be with you, for the Lord will greatly bless you.'

Mary was troubled and upset at the angel's words and she wondered what they meant. The angel said to Mary, 'Don't be afraid, Mary, God is pleased with you. You will have a son and you will call him Jesus. He will be great, he will be the Son of God. The Lord will make him a king just as David was, and he will rule Israel for ever, and his kingdom will never end.'

Mary was puzzled. She said to the angel, 'How can this happen? I am a virgin.'

The angel answered, 'The Holy Spirit will come down from heaven and God's power will come over you, and the child that you will bear will be called the Son of God. Remember, nothing is impossible for God.'

Mary said, 'I am the Lord's servant. Let it happen just as you have said.' And the angel went away.

Assembly 3

Themes: Showing our values/Gabriel's message

Painting: The Annunciation
by Duccio

You will need:
- A pile of junk mail and letters
- A wastepaper bin
- Copies printed on paper of the letters provided **[O S3a,b]**, cut up and each placed in an envelope (optional)
- Four carrier bags to hold the printed letters (optional)
- Image of **The Annunciation [O P3/4]**

Introduction

We can learn something about a person by the letters they receive.

> **Older pupils**
> *Give individual pupils (or groups of pupils) four carrier bags containing the letters. (Teachers may wish to add more mail of their own creation.) Explain that each carrier bag contains the mail received by one person. Ask the pupils what they can deduce about each person from the mail they receive. The bags should contain the following:*
>
> *Bag 1 – letters 1–3*
> *Bag 2 – letters 4–6*
> *Bag 3 – letters 7–9*
> *Bag 4 – letters 10–12*

Alternative: *The above activity can be done by the teacher.*

If a person's mail consists of lots of unpaid bills, they may be forgetful. If their mail is made up of party invitations and information about films and concerts, they probably have a busy social life. If their mail contains lots of information about business matters, they may have a busy job. If their mail contains letters from important people, they may be well known themselves. Today's story centres on a message and what it says about the person who received it.

> **Younger pupils**
> *Start the assembly by asking pupils to help you sort your mail. Comment on each item as you pick it up. Bin junk mail with the appropriate comment. Make sure there is at least one letter that is important because of who wrote it and what it contains.*

Go through your mail. Not all written messages are important; some we put straight in the bin. *Ask pupils what makes us decide whether a message goes in the bin or whether we take notice of it.* We keep messages that are important; we also keep letters from someone who matters to us. The story in this assembly centres on a message and how Mary responded to it.

Core material

Show the painting. In the painting we see the angel Gabriel delivering a message to Mary. He arrives at a small town in Galilee called Nazareth. Duccio has painted it like an Italian house, as he would not have known what type of house Mary lived in. He has painted Gabriel carrying the staff of a royal messenger, for he carries a message from the King – a title Christians use for God. This is not the sort of message you bin. *Read the biblical material.* Gabriel delivers the message personally, not by letter. This was more personal and also took account of the fact that Mary probably would not have been able to read. Girls did not go to school in first-century Israel. However, Mary is often shown with a book – the Bible – as an indication that the Bible foretold the coming of Jesus.

If we judged Mary by the 'mail' or messages she received on this occasion we would think her very important. But she was an ordinary girl. She gathers her cloak round her in fear. She is not used to important visitors. This mismatch between the importance of the message and the status of Mary matters to Christians. They believe it says something about God's values. In the Bible God often chooses the people that others reject, showing that to him they are important.

Something to think about

The way we treat others shows our values. People cannot see our values, they are invisible – just as our thoughts are. People can only see values when they are put into action, just as Christians detect God's values in his choice of Mary.

Optional prayer

People do not know what we are like on the inside,
Only you know that, God.
Help us to express our values
By what we say,
By what we do,
And by the way we treat people.

Music suggestions

'The Angel Gabriel from Heaven Came', *The Shorter New Oxford Book of Carols*, edited by H. Keyte and A. Parrott (Oxford University Press, 1993).
'The Virgin Mary had a baby boy', www.carolsing. com/cn-virgin-mary-had-a-baby-boy.html

Assembly 4

Themes: Plans for the future/The cost of saying 'yes' for Mary

Painting: The Annunciation
by Duccio

You will need:
- Image of **The Annunciation** [**O** P3/4]

Introduction

It is very hard to break a piece of news to someone when you know it is going to affect their whole life. We often turn over in our minds how on earth we are going to do it without upsetting the person involved. It is equally difficult to receive such news. People react in different ways: some people get angry, others go quiet, some get upset.

Drama option
Pupils can perform several 30-second sketches on delivering and receiving important news, illustrating the different ways in which people deliver news and react to it. Teachers should make up items of news suitable for the age of their pupils. For example: you didn't pass your exam, your friend is moving house, you have been chosen to represent the school at an important event. The examples should include a mixture of good and bad news.

Alternative
Ask pupils to think about the way they would react to each piece of news mentioned above.

Core material

The angel Gabriel had a similar problem. His news changed Mary's life for ever. *Read the biblical material.*

> **Older pupils**
> *Some teachers may wish to omit the story. Go to the section marked *.*
>
> **Younger pupils**
> *Read the story below, in which Bob Hartman explores Gabriel's dilemma.*

'The Surprise' by B. Hartman

Gabriel hugged his knees and scrunched himself back into the corner. He hated these surprise visits and that's all there was to it. The girl was whistling now. Doing her ordinary, everyday chores – as if this was some ordinary everyday, and not the most extraordinary day of her life.

The angel rested his chin on his knees. Think, Gabriel, think, he muttered to himself. She's young. But she's probably fragile. So how do you do it? How do you tell her that God is about to change her whole life, without scaring her to death?

Mary began to sweep as she whistled. And as the dust motes danced in front of her broom, catching the sun and changing shape like dirty little clouds, Gabriel had an idea.

What about a vision? he asked himself. It always worked with the prophets. The dust rises and takes on the form of a man. 'Mary,' the dust-man says, 'you are going to be the mother of the Son of God!' Gabriel shook his head, then buried it in his arms. No, no, no, he decided. Still too spooky. And besides, all it takes is a strong breeze and the poor girl has to dust her house all over again!

It was too late now, anyway. Mary had put her broom away and was across the room preparing dinner. Gabriel climbed up out of the corner and stretched. Then he followed her to the table. Bread, she was making bread. And as she mixed the ingredients, another idea started to knead itself together and rise in Gabriel's head.

He would write a message in the flour on the table. Of course! An invisible hand, like the one that scratched those letters on the wall in Babylon. But it would have to be brief. It was a small table, after all. And there wasn't much time. Mary's parents were both gone, and there was no telling when they would be back. He wouldn't want to be surprised in the middle of his message. Gabriel hated surprises!

And then somebody knocked on the door. Gabriel jumped, startled by the sound. Mary quietly turned and walked to the door, wiping her hands as she went. It was a girl about Mary's age. Gabriel watched as they hugged and exchanged greetings. She had a brief message for Mary. It wasn't long before Mary said good-bye and shut the door again.

I could do that, Gabriel thought. Knock at the door like some unexpected visitor, and just give her the message ... But what if she got scared and slammed the door in my face? Or what if someone passed by and saw us? She'll have enough explaining to do when the baby comes. She won't need to make excuses for some mysterious stranger.

*Show the painting. Many artists have explored the way Gabriel broke his news and the way Mary received it. In the Bible, the angel tells Mary not to be afraid. In this painting by Duccio the angel is forceful. He strides into Mary's house and the hand may be raised in blessing but it is a very forceful gesture. There is no doubt that she is the chosen one. Such a choice can be threatening for it carries responsibility. The moment she says 'Yes' her life will change for good. Any dreams or plans she had for the future will change. **(cont.)**

Assembly 4 (continued)

Themes: Plans for the future/The cost of saying 'yes' for Mary

Draw a dream cloud and write in it some of the plans for the future which Mary may have had. In the first century, when teenage girls dreamt of the future they thought of marriage, children and the security of village life. We all have plans. Our plans might be different from Mary's but if something happens to take away those hopes and plans, something inside us dies: it is like a mini-death, the death of a dream.

What is Mary's reaction to the angel's news? The book drops to her side. She shields herself with her cloak. Her hand is over her heart. Is it fear? Is she thinking it over and counting the cost to herself? Is she saying one last good-bye to those plans? This painting has captured something of the cost of saying 'Yes'. This is not a confident 'take-on-the-world' type of Mary. This is an unsure young girl taking on a responsibility.

Something to think about

Look at the pointing fingers of the angel. Think of a time when you were chosen for something. Was it easy to say 'Yes' or did being chosen involve you in responsibility? Look at Mary's face and her reaction. Think of some of the hopes and plans you have for your life. She gave up her plans. If she had said 'No' we would probably never have heard about this girl from Nazareth. Sometimes our hopes and plans don't come true: that does not mean there is not another future in store.

Optional prayer

We face many mini-deaths in life – not the death of people, but the death of hopes and dreams. Help us, Lord, to know when it is right to 'bury' those dreams and to turn and face a new future.

Music suggestions

'Who came to Mary?' *Big Blue Planet,* edited by J. Jarvis (Stainer & Bell Ltd and Methodist Church Division of Education and Youth, 1995).
'An angel came from Heaven', *A Year of Celebration,* by J. Porter and J. MacCrimmon (MacCrimmon).

The Adoration of the Shepherds

by Guido Reni (1575–1642)

Background to the painting

Date: about 1640

Medium: oil on canvas

Dimensions: 480 cm x 321 cm

Guido Reni (*Gwee-doh Rray-nee*) was an influential painter of the seventeenth century who worked in Bologna. Reni was influenced by the art of Classical Rome and the painter Raphael. He studied Roman statues, busts and cameos for his models. A modest and religious man (he attended church daily), Reni was, however, addicted to gambling, which caused severe financial problems and led to his studio making many copies of his paintings. Reni did not aim for realism in his paintings: he painted nature 'improved'. He portrayed an idealized beauty which often expressed deep religious emotion. In this painting, the shepherds come to worship Jesus. The angels' scroll reads 'Glory to God in the highest' (in Latin). Reni painted this scene twice. The other version (an altarpiece) can be seen in the Certosa di S. Martino in Naples. No one knows which one was painted first.

Biblical material

Luke 2:8–20 – The shepherds

On the night that Jesus was born, some shepherds in the fields near Bethlehem were looking after their sheep. Suddenly an angel appeared to them and a bright light shone around them. The shepherds were terrified. But the angel said, 'Don't be frightened. I have good news for you. News which will bring joy to everyone. This day, in Bethlehem, a Saviour has been born. He is Christ the Lord. You will find him wrapped in swaddling clothes and lying in a manger.' Suddenly the sky was full of angels singing, 'Glory to God in the highest and on earth peace, goodwill to all people.'

After the angels had left, the shepherds hurried to Bethlehem and found Mary and Joseph and the baby just as the angels had said to them. The shepherds told Mary and Joseph what the angel had said. Everyone listened and was surprised, but Mary remembered all these things and wondered what they meant. The shepherds left the stable and returned to their sheep, praising God.

Matthew 2:1–16 – The wise men

After Jesus was born, wise men from the east came to Jerusalem and asked King Herod where the new King of the Jews could be found, for they had seen his star in the east. When Herod heard this he was worried. He called together his advisors and they told him the King of the Jews would be born in Bethlehem.

Herod asked the wise men how long ago the star had appeared. Then he sent them to Bethlehem, asking them to return and tell him where the young child was so that he too could worship him. The wise men followed the star until they came to Bethlehem. It stopped over the house where the child lay. The wise men entered and found Jesus with Mary, his mother. They bowed down and worshipped, presenting their gifts of gold, frankincense and myrrh. After this they returned to their own country, having been warned by God not to return to Herod.

Joseph was also warned by God to take Mary and Jesus and escape to Egypt, for Herod, angry at being tricked by the wise men, had sent out orders for all the boys in Bethlehem of two years old and under to be killed.

Assembly 5

Themes: Remembering the homeless and refugees/Facing the realities of Christmas

Painting: The Adoration of the Shepherds
by Guido Reni

You will need:
- Some DVDs: a U certificate, a PG and a suitable 15+ (optional)
- Gold or silver tinsel (optional)
- Image of **The Adoration of the Shepherds [O P5/6]**

Introduction

> **Younger pupils**
> *Ask how many pupils have been in nativity plays. What parts did they play? (Use only the U and PG material below.)*
>
> **Older pupils**
> *Ask them to think back to when they were in nativity plays as infants. Option: bring in a tinsel halo and wear it yourself. Ask how many were angels as infants.*

Read the biblical material – both the story of the shepherds and the story of the wise men. Show the DVD covers (optional). If the Christmas story was turned into a DVD, what rating would it have? Would it be a U, a PG or a 15+? *Read the reviews below or ask pupils to read them, holding a suitable DVD cover.*

The Christmas story: rating U. This is a gentle story about the birth of Jesus. It is a warm story about Mary's courage and Joseph's devotion. The animals in the stable and, of course, the baby will appeal to children. The scruffy shepherds and the richness of the kings add humour and contrast. A must for any child.

The Christmas story: rating PG. This heart-warming story of love and courage will interest the older child. There are scenes of poverty and some violence which younger children might find distressing. However, the main themes of the story are love and peace. Parents need to use their judgement when taking a child to see this film.

The Christmas story: rating 15+. This hard-hitting story of love in the face of hardship and hatred continues to appeal. The birth scenes in the filthy conditions of the stable are graphically shot. The same is true of the massacre of the children and the flight of Jesus and his family as refugees with Herod's assassins close on their heels. This is not a film for the squeamish.

Often we turn Christmas into a U rating when really it is a PG or15+. We forget it is about a poor couple forced to travel to Bethlehem by orders of the occupying power – the Romans. Mary and Joseph were homeless in Bethlehem and Mary gave birth in a stable. They then became refugees as they fled to Egypt from Herod's murderous soldiers.

Core material

Show the painting. The artist, Guido Reni, has painted a traditional image of the first Christmas. Everything is bathed in a gentle light which centres on the baby. This is the Christmas story painted as a U-rated film. Guido Reni was a very popular artist in the eighteenth and nineteenth centuries. Many of his paintings have found their way on to Christmas cards. This is often how our nativity plays present the scene. Just visible in the background, however, is the stable. It is deep in shadow, for this is the unpleasant side of Christmas – Jesus was homeless. Mary herself is young in this painting: she may have been a teenage mother. The shepherds grouped around the manger look respectable enough, but hired shepherds were the outcasts of their day. This gentle scene masks a deeper and darker reality – the PG/15 aspect of the Christmas story. Looking at the darker side of Christmas is a way of reminding Christians that it is an appropriate time to remember the homeless, the refugees and those people who are lonely or rejected. That was as much part of the first Christmas as shepherds and angels.

Something to think about

Think about those for whom Christmas is a difficult time, people who are lonely or homeless or those who are refugees. A time which focuses on families and friends makes loneliness and homelessness even harder to bear.

Optional prayer

Christmas is a time when we think of being at home and sharing the celebration with our families and friends. The homeless have no homes, and refugees are sometimes far from their families. Help us, God, not to forget the homeless and the refugees at Christmas. In the name of him who was both homeless and a refugee.

Music suggestions

'The shepherds were excited', *Children's Praise*, compiled by P. Burt et al. (Marshall Pickering, 1991).
'Cold Frosty Night', *A Year of Celebration*, by J. Porter and J. MacCrimmon (MacCrimmon).

Assembly 6

Themes: Time to stop and think/What Christmas is all about

Painting: The Adoration of the Shepherds
by Guido Reni

You will need:
- Copy of the Christmas action list [O S6] (if required)
- Paper and pens
- Items/pictures for the poem (optional)
- Image of **The Adoration of the Shepherds [O P5/6]**

Introduction

Younger pupils
Ask pupils to create a list of the things you have to do for Christmas, or use the one provided.

Older pupils
Create a list as above and comment on how much there is to do for Christmas. When does a teacher find time to shop, cook and get ready for a party? Put forward a case for a month's holiday at Christmas in order to get everything ready.

Core material

The emphasis at Christmas is on food, presents and parties. This makes it a busy time as we put a lot of effort into preparing those things. The poet Gordon Bailey has written this poem about the way in which Christmas is celebrated. *Read the poem but omit lines 8, 10 and 12 with younger pupils. Pupils could each read one line as they hold up a suitable object (optional).*

Gone and Forgotten
Cardmas.
Crackermas.
Tinselmas.
Jinglemas.
Turkeymas.
Puddingmas.
Stockingmas.
Drunkenmas.
Excitementmas.
Overdraftmas.
Disappointmentmas.
Alkaseltzermas!

God came down at CHRISTmas
and found it wasn't.

Show the painting. The artist, Guido Reni, has painted a picture of the birth of Jesus according to the Gospel of Luke. *Read the biblical material.* In this painting, nothing much is happening. Mary cradles the baby; Joseph sits, his hands clasped in prayer; the shepherds kneel in worship. It is a moment of quiet, except for the singing of the angels. The artist has indicated this by the scroll the angels are holding, which reads, 'Glory to God in the highest'. It is a picture of worship. The artist has reminded Christians that, for them, this is what Christmas is all about. He has done this in a number of ways:

Jesus is the centre of attention in the painting.
He is surrounded by light.
Everybody's gaze and worship is directed towards him.

For this type of celebration of Christmas, a very different sort of preparation is necessary: it happens on the inside. It involves stopping and thinking about the important things in life.

Something to think about

Ask pupils to consider making time this Christmas to think about the important things in life. If possible, arrange for a pupil to read out their own poem, written beforehand, about the first Christmas, using 'Gone and Forgotten' as a model. An example is given below.

Shepherdmas
Kingmas
Starmas
Angelmas
Stablemas
Journeymas
Lovemas
Noelmas
Mangermas
Mothermas
Worshipmas
Holymas

God came down that Christmas.

(Rachel Walker)

Optional prayer

In the busyness of buying,
Remind us of Christmas.
In the pressure of parties,
Remind us of Christmas.
In the hassle of the holiday,
Remind us of Christmas and give us your peace.

Music suggestions

'Rise up, Shepherd', *Come and Praise*, compiled by G. Marshall-Taylor and D. Coombes (BBC, 1996).
'While shepherds watched', most traditional hymn books.

The Marriage at Cana

by Mattia Preti (1613–1699)

Background to the painting

Date: about 1655–60

Medium: oil on canvas

Dimensions: 203.2 cm x 226 cm

Mattia Preti (*Mah-tee-ah Preh-tee*) was born in Taverna in Italy but he made his mark as an artist in Naples. In 1656, plague killed a large number of artists in Naples, but Mattia Preti survived and became a leading artist in the city. His dramatic style was popular and he was one of the important painters of the new Catholic spirituality (Counter Reformation) of the seventeenth century.

In 1661, Preti moved to Malta, where he contributed paintings to a large number of churches in the city of Valletta. Preti was a member of the Knights of St John, who ruled Malta, and he received many commissions from them. (Their symbol can be seen in the Maltese Cross used by the St John Ambulance brigade.)

This is a painting of Jesus' first miracle. He is shown at the right, next to the Virgin Mary. Preti painted this subject several times during his sojourn in Naples. This version may have been painted for the Perrelli family. At the time that Preti was painting, people made links between different parts of the Bible. One part of the Bible was seen as a 'hint' of a later event. This is called 'prefiguring'. The wine in this story prefigures (hints at) the wine of the Last Supper (Eucharist/Communion).

 ## Biblical material

John 2:1–11

Mary, Jesus and all his disciples had been invited to a wedding which was taking place at Cana in Galilee. When the wine had run out Mary said to Jesus, 'They don't have any more wine.' Jesus replied, 'Mother, the time's not right yet.' Mary then said to the servants, 'Do whatever Jesus says.'

The Jews were careful to wash before meals in a special way. For this purpose six large stone water jars were available. Each jar held over 100 litres. Jesus said to the servants, 'Fill the jars right to the top with water.' Then, when every jar was full, he said, 'Now take some of the water and give it to the man in charge.'

The servants obeyed and the man in charge drank some of the water that had now turned to wine. He didn't know where the wine came from but the servants did. He turned to the bridegroom and said, 'Most people serve the best wine first. Then, after the guests have had plenty to drink, the ordinary wine is served. But you kept the best wine until now.'

This was Jesus' first miracle, which occurred in the village of Cana in Galilee.

Assembly 7

Themes: Motives/Miracles

Painting: The Marriage at Cana

by Mattia Preti

You will need:
- A wedding DVD/video (optional)
- Paper and pens
- Script for 'The Waiter' [**O** S7] (optional)
- A mobile phone (optional)
- Image of **The Marriage at Cana** [**O** P7/8]

Introduction

Lots of things can go wrong with weddings, partly because it is a time when everyone is really desperate to get everything right. Ask pupils to list the things that can possibly go wrong.

> **Older pupils**
> *Show a DVD of someone's wedding and press the pause button at places where there could have been a disaster. Alternatively, show a DVD of wedding disasters or the scene where Charles forgets the ring in* Four Weddings and a Funeral. *If none of these is available, use the activity for younger pupils.*
>
> **Younger pupils**
> *If appropriate, ask some members of staff to share what went wrong at their weddings.*

Core material

Show the painting. In this painting, the artist, Mattia Preti, has shown us a disaster at a wedding. He worked in the days before DVDs, but this painting is the equivalent of a wedding-disaster DVD. In this wedding disaster, the dress is not ripped, the car doesn't break down and the best man does not lose the ring, but there is a disaster. *Read the biblical material.*

Unlike a DVD, the artist can show us only one scene at a time. He has chosen the moment when the servant offers a glass of the newly created wine to the best man. The best man sits on one side of the table, reaching out his hand to take the glass; Jesus sits on the other side of the table, opposite him, with his hand pointing to the large jars. Between the two hands, Christians believe that a miracle took place.

Drama option
The drama 'The Waiter' can be performed here or it can be pre-recorded.

Alternative
Look at a variety of motives that impel us to do things. Ask pupils for examples of some of the following motives in practice. For example, we might treat someone well because we are told to not because we want to.

want	pride	ambition
love	to impress	feel it's the
necessity (legal)	fear or because	right thing
need	someone	to do
hate	makes us	
enjoyment	feeling sorry	
guilt	for someone	

The important people in this painting are the servants, the ones with their backs to us, for they are the only people, other than Jesus, who know what has happened. This is Jesus' first miracle and it is an unusual one. Healing and teaching would seem more in keeping with the rest of Jesus' life than creating a large quantity of wine. Why did he do it? What was his motive? *If you have used the list of motives, go through these and ask pupils to decide which one applies.*

The answer lies in the customs of the day. Weddings were important events. The celebrations could last for up to two weeks and wine was the main drink – it was safer than water, which might be impure. Hospitality was very highly valued in the Middle East, so the wine running out at a wedding would have been a real disaster.

Jesus was very reluctant to perform this miracle and he keeps very quiet about it afterwards, so his motive could not have been a desire to draw attention to himself or to impress. Christians believe that he turned the water into wine in response to a situation that would have upset the bride and groom and their family, who may have been family friends. His very first miracle was to save the feelings of an ordinary couple. Looked at like this, it is in keeping with the rest of his life.

Something to think about

Motives are difficult to untangle. Sometimes we do the right thing from the wrong motive. Often, we do not know why we do things. Think about the last time you helped someone. Did you act out of care, or was it to impress?

Optional prayer

Is it what we do that matters, or why we do it, or both? You who see the heart, unravel our motives and help us to put them right.

Music suggestions

'Oh no, the wine's all gone!' *Children's Praise*, compiled by P. Burt et al. (Marshall Pickering, 1991).
'Jesus turned water into wine', *Wake Up, World!*, compiled by M. Forster and C. Tambling (Kevin Mayhew, 1993).

Assembly 8

Themes: Privacy/Jesus sacrificing his privacy

Painting: The Marriage at Cana
by Mattia Preti

You will need:
- Paper and pens
- Wedding photographs (optional)
- A wedding dress and veil or a bridesmaid's dress (optional)
- Image of **The Marriage at Cana [O P7/8]**

Introduction

> **Younger pupils**
> *List the items needed in a traditional Western 'white' wedding. If possible, show a dress and veil. Ask which pupils have been to a wedding and whether any of them have ever been bridesmaids or page boys.*

Note: *Teachers may wish to explain that this 'Christian-type' wedding is only one type of traditional ceremony. Pupils may like to share details of other wedding celebrations.*

> **Older pupils**
> A Western 'white' wedding has a number of traditional ingredients. *Ask pupils to suggest items needed and write their responses on paper or acetate, or use the list below.*

bride	confetti
bridegroom	wedding cake
best man	wedding car
bridesmaids	flowers
long white dress	veil

The wedding sometimes takes place in a church and is followed by a reception at which there is food and lots of speeches. A great deal of preparation goes into making sure that everything runs smoothly.

Core material

Show the painting and read the biblical material.

> **Younger pupils**
> *Select from the information below and replace/explain any difficult words.*

Mattia Preti, like many artists, painted biblical scenes. However, the stories of the Bible give little detail about what people wore, the houses they lived in or what they ate. To make up for this, artists filled in the detail using their imaginations and clothed most of the people in their paintings as people of their own times.

The bride
As we can see, the bride, who is on the left, does not wear white. She just wears her best clothes and everybody else wears theirs. White wedding dresses are quite a modern trend. The bride in the biblical story would have worn her best clothes and a veil over her face. She may have worn an embroidered white dress for white clothes were popular as best clothes in biblical times.

The guests
Jesus was invited to the wedding along with his disciples and his mother. The disciples would have counted as part of Jesus' family. Jesus may have been standing in for Joseph, who had probably died. He accompanied Mary as her eldest son.

The food
The food in the painting is not a Middle Eastern feast of the first century but an Italian one of the seventeenth century. In biblical times wedding food was provided by the family and guests. Jesus would have been expected to contribute food.

The reception
The wedding was a local one, for it took place in Galilee where Jesus was brought up. Wedding parties could go on for a week or even two: that was why they would have needed a large amount of wine. In Israel, the bridegroom would walk from his own home to his future bride's home, collect the bride and bring her back to his house. It was there that the meal would have taken place, not in a hotel. The marriage feast may well have taken place at night, as Mattia Preti has depicted on this occasion.

Stone jars
The stone jars would have probably held over a hundred litres. They contained hand-washing water, for Jews were required to wash their hands in a special way before meals.

The wine
Wine was the main drink in the Middle East. It was safer than water and was particularly used for celebrations. For the wine to run out would have been a breach of hospitality: the hosts would have been letting down their guests.

The Bible says that Jesus was reluctant to perform this miracle. For thirty years, he had lived unknown as a carpenter in Nazareth but this miracle catapulted him into the public eye. Miracles do tend to get you noticed! In the painting, everyone stares down the table at what is happening. As soon as that glass of wine, which the servant is holding, is tasted, Jesus will never again be a private person. Crowds will follow him everywhere. What we see in this painting is the split second between Jesus the unknown carpenter and Jesus the popular figure. From this moment on, he will have little time to himself. His time will be spent responding to the needs of the sick, the sorrowing and the rejected people of society. Part of the price he paid for caring was the loss of his privacy.

Something to think about

Ask pupils to think about popular characters and their first moment of fame. This painting is like a glimpse of an unknown footballer's last moment on the bench before he scores a winning goal. It is the 'star' shopping unrecognized in the supermarket the day before the hit record is released.

Privacy is something most of us guard. Sometimes we are called upon to give up time when we want to be by ourselves. Giving up time and privacy is often harder than giving money.

Optional prayer

Commitment to others comes at a cost. The price is paid in time and privacy. Help us, Lord, to spend our time and not just our money on others.

Music suggestions

'Oh no, the wine's all gone!', *Children's Praise*, compiled by P. Burt et al. (Marshall Pickering, 1991).
'Jesus turned water into wine', *Wake Up, World!*, compiled by M. Forster and C. Tambling (Kevin Mayhew, 1993).

Christ teaching from Saint Peter's Boat on the Lake of Gennesaret

by Herman Saftleven (1609–1685)

Background to the painting

Date: 1667

Medium: oil on oak

Dimensions: 46.7 cm x 62.8 cm

Herman Saftleven (*Hair-man Saft-lay-ven*) came from a family of painters. His father, brothers and his daughter were also artists. Herman Saftleven was based in Utrecht, Holland, and between 1630 and 1684 he produced about 300 paintings. He worked for the leading Dutch family, the House of Orange, and in his lifetime he was one of the best-known Dutch painters. Saftleven painted large hilly landscapes, often with craggy rocks in the background. The people in his paintings are small but painted with precision. This painting reflects Luke 5:1–3. The same subject was painted by the artist in 1666 and can be seen in Edinburgh, in the National Gallery of Scotland. Inscribed bottom left on a rock is Herman Saftleven's monogram (HS) and the date (1667).

Biblical material

Luke 5:1–3 – Jesus preaches from a boat

Jesus was teaching the people by Lake Gennesaret (also known as Lake Galilee). The people crowded around him for they were eager to hear what he had to say about God. Nearby were two boats, left there by local fishermen who had gone to wash their nets. Jesus got into one of the boats – it belonged to a man called Simon – and asked him to push it out into deeper water so that it stood just off the shore. Jesus sat down in the boat and taught the people who crowded on the shore.

Mark 1:16–20 – Jesus chooses his first disciples

As Jesus was walking along the shore of Lake Galilee he saw Simon and his brother Andrew; they were fishermen and they were casting their nets into the lake. Jesus said to them, 'Come with me and I will teach you how to bring in people instead of fish.' Right then the two brothers dropped their nets and went with him. Jesus walked on and soon he saw James and John, the sons of Zebedee. They too were in a boat, mending their nets. At once Jesus asked them to come with him. They left their father in the boat with the hired workers and went with him.

Extra biblical material

Matthew 20:1–15 – 'The Workers in the Vineyard'

Jesus said that God is generous, like the owner in this story.

Early one morning the owner of a vineyard went out to hire some workers to pick his grapes. He agreed to pay them the usual amount for a day's work and then he sent them off to start work.

At about nine o'clock that same morning, he saw some other men standing around with nothing to do. He said he would pay them what was fair if they would help to pick his grapes, so they too worked in his vineyard.

At midday, and again at about three o'clock in the afternoon, he hired more workers for there were always men standing around with nothing to do. Finally at about five in the afternoon, one hour before work finished for the day, the owner found some men loafing about in the market place. He said to them 'Why have you been standing here all day doing nothing?' 'Because no one hired us,' they answered. So he hired them and sent them to work in his vineyard.

At six o'clock the owner of the vineyard told the man in charge of the workers to tell the men to collect their wages. He gave out the wages himself, beginning with those who had only worked one hour. These men were given a full day's pay. On seeing this, those who had worked longer thought they would get paid more, but they were given the same. They began to grumble. 'Those who only worked one hour got paid the same as us and yet we've been working all day in the hot sun.' The owner looked at them sadly and said, 'My friends, have I cheated you? I paid you a fair wage, as we agreed. Now take your money and go! It's none of your business if I decide to be generous. It's up to me what I do with my money.'

Luke 14:16–24 – 'The Great Feast'

Jesus said that God welcomes everyone, like the man in this story.

A man once gave a great feast and invited lots of people to it. When everything was ready he sent his servants to tell the guests to come. However, each guest made an excuse. The first one said, 'I have just bought some land and I need to check it, so I won't be able to come.' The next guest excused himself by saying, 'I have just bought some new animals. I need to try them out. I won't be able to come.' Another guest said, 'I've just got married, so I definitely won't be there.'

When the servant told his master what had happened the master became angry and ordered his servant to go into every street and alley in town and invite those who were poor, blind or unable to walk to his party. The servant returned and said, 'Sir, your orders have been carried out, but there's still plenty of room.' The master replied, 'Go into the countryside and bring as many people as you can so that my house is full. Not one of the original guests will taste my dinner!'

Assembly 9

Themes: Including people/Jesus, the teacher who shocked

Painting: Christ teaching from Saint Peter's Boat on the Lake of Gennesaret
by Herman Saftleven

You will need:
- Scripts for 'The Workers in the Vineyard' [**O** S9a,b] and 'The Great Feast' [**O** S9c,d] (for drama option)
- A party invitation (enlarged)
- A membership card for a club or other organization
- PE hoop (younger pupils)
- Image of **Christ teaching from Saint Peter's Boat** [**O** P9/10]

Introduction

We often think about going to see a band or a film *(ask for suggestions)*. Not many people rush to hear someone teaching. Pupils do not hammer on classroom doors to get in, hoping to hear a teacher. That was not so in Jesus' day. People came to listen to new teachers if they had something unusual, or even shocking, to say. But if you wanted to hear someone speak you often had to travel, and be part of a very large crowd. *Read Luke 5:1-3.*

Core material

Show the painting. In this painting by Herman Saftleven, we see Jesus teaching the people. The crowds, although painted in miniature, fill the shore. More lurk in the shadowy area beneath the rocks. Jesus has to climb into a boat which we can see in the front of the picture. The surrounding countryside looks bleak – craggy rocks and trees clinging to cliffs under a cloudy sky. What was it that brought so many people to this inhospitable place to listen to him? The answer was his stories and his unusual teaching. *Read either 'The Great Feast' or 'The Workers in the Vineyard' or split this assembly over two days and use both. Separate notes are supplied to enable you to do this.*

Drama option
Use one or both of the scripts provided. These can be performed during the assembly by a group of pupils, or they can be pre-recorded.

Alternative

> **Younger pupils**
> *Display a large party invitation when telling the Parable of the Great Feast.*
>
> **Older pupils**
> *Use an ordinary-sized invitation. Discuss how it feels when people don't turn up to a party.*

The Parable of the Workers in the Vineyard
If you are using this story, talk about fair and minimum wages. Ask what the rate of pay is for a paper round. How would you feel if you only did part of the round and got paid the whole sum? How would you feel if you did the whole round and others only did part of it and you all got paid the same? *Talk about the difference between fairness and generosity. Explain that generosity is being more than fair, not less than fair.* The Bible records that Jesus taught about God in a way that shocked people. He likened God to an employer who was ridiculously generous and gave people more than they deserved: this is expressed in the Parable of the Workers in the Vineyard. Jesus taught in a way that the people could understand. They knew what it was like to be out of work and desperate. The people in authority, however, thought he went too far. They wanted a stricter God – a God who was a bit more cautious, not this generous God Jesus described.

The Parable of the Great Feast
Jesus likened God to someone who gave a party and threw it open to everyone, even the local down-and-outs. The crowds loved it. Suddenly, here was someone talking about God in a way they understood. Some of them knew what it was like to be homeless, and the picture of God Jesus painted in the stories he told attracted people. However, not everyone liked Jesus' teaching. Some of the religious leaders were very shocked indeed. It did not seem right to them that God should accept just anyone. They thought that following God should be like a select club with membership cards *(show your card)*. They wanted rules and regulations.

Something to think about

Imagine a circle in your mind *(use a PE hoop with younger pupils)*. We often want to draw circles small and include only people like us inside the circle of our friends. Jesus shocked people by drawing the circle wide and including everyone.

Optional prayer

Often we want to tame Jesus, make him sensible, tone down his teaching. But he remains untamed, and his teaching still shocks, 2000 years on. Lord, stop us from trying to lock your words in a prison of niceness.

Music suggestions

'Break out' and 'God has put a circle around us', *Big Blue Planet,* edited by J. Jarvis (Stainer & Bell and Methodist Church Division of Education and Youth, 1995).
'The wedding banquet', *A Year of Celebration,* by J. Porter and J. MacCrimmon (MacCrimmon).

Assembly 10

Themes: Potential/The disciples

Painting: Christ teaching from Saint Peter's Boat on the Lake of Gennesaret
by Herman Saftleven

You will need:

- Gift wrap and newspaper (younger pupils)
- A variety of items in different packaging, e.g. 'economy ranges', and fancy packaging (older pupils)
- 'The Apostles' Rap' on page 45 (for music option)
- Image of **Christ teaching from Saint Peter's Boat** [**O** P9/10]

Introduction

Younger pupils
Show the newspaper and the gift wrap. Ask pupils what they would wrap with the gift wrap and what they would wrap with the newspaper. Can you always tell a present by the way it is wrapped?

Older pupils
Show the different types of packaging. Explain that some items have minimal packaging to save money, while others are designed to attract the shopper. The product inside might be the same. Which do you prefer? Would your choice be swayed by the packaging?

Core material

Show the painting. The artist, Herman Saftleven, has shown Jesus as very small in a huge landscape. You have to look very hard to find Jesus. He does not look impressive. This Jesus was a man who wanted to change the world, but he looks small and insignificant in this painting. He is dwarfed by the hills around him. In the first century, Jesus was an insignificant person in the world population. But you can't always judge someone by the way they appear. Only a few years after his death, people complained that Jesus' followers were 'turning the world upside down'. When Jesus was alive they had not seen the potential of this ordinary-looking man.

The artist shows us the occasion when Jesus chooses Simon (also known as Peter) as his first disciple. This was the first part of Jesus' plan to change the world. He chose twelve followers. We might think he would choose the bravest, the brightest and the best, but when we look at his choice of followers he seems to have chosen a mixed bag of unknown and unexceptional men.

The Bible records that Jesus started by choosing four fishermen – Simon Peter, his brother Andrew, James and John. *Read Mark 1:16–20.* They certainly would not have been anybody else's first choices for a band of men to change the world. The rest of Jesus' disciples were just as ordinary. Matthew was a tax man, Simon Zealotes was a freedom fighter. We know nothing about Thaddaeus or James the Younger – except that presumably James was younger than someone else. We know that Nathaniel (also known as Bartholomew) was honest and Judas was not – he stole money. We know Philip was Nathaniel's friend and we know Thomas had a twin.

Music option
The rap on page 45 can be performed here. Use the rap rhythm on the keyboard to establish the beat. The rap can be pre-recorded.

Alternative
Read the rap as a poem.

When Jesus first started travelling around Galilee with his twelve disciples, the Romans probably did not quake in their boots. A few years later, however, the Romans knew they had cause to fear. Jesus saw the potential in these men, even though other people would have dismissed them. He didn't look at the packaging, he looked at the person and saw the potential. Later events were to prove him right. That group of followers led a revolutionary movement that rocked the Roman world.

Something to think about

Look at the wrapping paper and the newspaper. Sometimes we think a lot of ourselves and think we are a shiny-wrap type of person. At other times we feel bad about ourselves and think we deserve nothing more than newspaper. This story is about forgetting the wrapping and looking at the real us – what is good about us and all that we could be. It is about seeing our potential, and other people's.

Optional prayer

Help us, Father, not to be over-anxious about what other people think of us.
Help us, Father, not to worry about the impression we are making.
You see us as we really are, and accept us.

Music suggestions

'The wedding banquet', *A Year of Celebration,* by J. Porter and J. MacCrimmon (MacCrimmon).
'Jesus had all kinds of friends', *The Children's Hymn Book,* by K. Mayhew (Kevin Mayhew, 1997).

Christ addressing a Kneeling Woman

by Paolo Veronese (1528–1588)

Background to the painting

Date: about 1546

Medium: oil (identified) on canvas

Dimensions: 117.5 cm x 163.5 cm

Paolo Veronese *(Pow-loh Vee-rroh-nay-zee)* painted altarpieces, portraits and religious, mythological and historical works. He was born in Verona but did much of his work in Venice. His paintings are marked by their use of sumptuous but delicate colours (pale blue, silvery white, orange, lemon yellow) and the clear daylight which lights them. This is probably an early work of Veronese, painted in Verona. The kneeling woman was once thought to be Mary Magdalene or the woman taken in adultery because of the necklace she seems to be discarding. It is now thought to be the woman with a haemorrhage. It is very similar to a painting by Veronese of Christ raising the daughter of Jairus. Both miracles are rarely depicted by Western painters.

Biblical material

Mark 5:21–43 – Two healings

Jesus was standing on the shore of Lake Galilee when the head of the local synagogue, a man called Jairus, came up to him. Jairus knelt at Jesus' feet and begged him for help. 'My daughter is about to die,' he said. 'Please come and heal her.' Jesus went with him straight away and a great crowd followed him.

Amongst the crowd that were following him was a woman. She had suffered from a haemorrhage for twelve years. She had gone to many doctors, but instead of getting better she had got worse, and she had paid out all the money she had. The woman had heard about Jesus and so she crept up behind him, hidden in the crowd, and just touched the edge of Jesus' clothes. She said to herself, 'Maybe if I can just touch him I will get well.' And as soon as she touched him the bleeding stopped. She knew she was well.

When the woman touched him Jesus felt the power go out of him. He turned round and said, 'Who touched my clothes?' His disciples looked at him, puzzled. 'There are crowds all around you,' they said. 'Lots of people have touched you.' But Jesus turned round to see who had touched him in a special way. The woman knew what had happened. She came shaking with fear and knelt down in front of him and she told him her whole story. Jesus said to the woman, 'You're well now because of your faith. Go in peace.'

While Jesus was still speaking men from Jairus' home had come. 'Your daughter has died,' they said. 'Don't bother the teacher any more.' Jesus heard what they said but turned to Jairus and said, 'Don't worry, trust me.' Jesus took Peter, James and John and together they went to Jairus' home, where the mourners were already making a lot of noise. When Jesus arrived he said, 'Why are you crying and carrying on like this? The child isn't dead, she is only asleep.' But they laughed at him.

Jesus sent them all out of the house except the girl's father and mother and with the three disciples went to see the girl. He took her by the hand and said, 'Talitha koum', which means 'Little girl, get up.' And she got up and walked around. Everybody was astonished but Jesus ordered them not to tell anyone, and then told them to give her something to eat.

Assembly 11

Themes: Character/Jairus' daughter

Painting: Christ addressing a Kneeling Woman
by Paolo Veronese

You will need:
- Wallpaper and pens or enlarged copy of the outline of a person [O S11]
- Image of **Christ addressing a Kneeling Woman** [O P11/12]

Introduction

Younger pupils
Ask someone to lie down on the wallpaper with their feet together. Draw round them. Display the outline and ask pupils to invent a name for your imaginary person. Ask them how we could tell what the person was like. How could we find out about his/her character? Write their suggestions in the outline.

Older pupils
As above, using the outline provided.

Core material

Read the biblical material. This story is about two miracles which Christians believe Jesus performed. The first miracle involved the healing of a woman who had been ill for twelve years. The second miracle involved a twelve-year-old girl. These two women had little in common. One had spent all her money on doctors and was now poor. The girl was the daughter of a religious leader who may have been quite prosperous. A lively twelve-year-old had little in common with a sick middle-aged woman.

At twelve, Jairus' daughter was almost a woman, for people could be engaged at twelve and married at thirteen. She was just entering the adult world and her life lay before her. But she had become seriously ill. There was not much these two women had shared up to now: they were from different generations. Now they shared illness. Illness does not care who it strikes – young or old, rich or poor. It does not discriminate – and neither did Jesus.

Show the painting. In this painting by Veronese, we see a crisis. The leader of the local synagogue, Jairus (possibly the man in white with a red turban), was an important man in the town. His twelve-year-old daughter was his only child. Jairus was desperate for Jesus to come to his house and help his daughter. In the painting we see him looking back in anguish when Jesus stops to heal the woman who we see kneeling in the centre of the painting. To Jairus, this healing was a sideline, something that happened on the way. His daughter was his main concern. By making the older woman the centre of the painting, however, the artist has shown that to Jesus she was anything but a sideline.

Jairus was desperate. Every minute counted. To him, Jesus was wasting time with this other woman. Then Jairus' worst nightmare came true. A servant arrived to say his daughter was dead. If Jesus had not delayed to heal this woman, his daughter might still be alive. But Jesus asked Jairus to trust him.

By the time Jesus arrived at Jairus' house, the funeral preparations had already begun. The mourners were already there. Jesus told them to go away, saying the child was asleep – which raised a laugh. They knew when someone was dead, for death was more of an everyday occurrence then. The Bible account says that he quietly went to the girl's room with just her parents and three disciples, and with the words 'Little girl, get up' he brought her back to life. Jesus promptly told the family to keep quiet about it. Publicity was the last thing this girl needed.

For Christians, this story is not only evidence of Jesus' power, it also tells Christians about his character. *Refer back to the introduction.* He not only spoke about people being important, he showed they were important to him by the way he treated them. He saw no difference between the daughter of the local synagogue leader and a sick older woman. He did not reject either of them because they were women, even though women were not considered very important then. A woman occupies the centre of this painting.

Something to think about

We are sending messages about our character to other people all the time, by what we say, what we do and how we relate to others. People judge us by the evidence we give them. Sometimes what we say and what we do do not match. People are more likely to take notice of what we do rather than what we say.

Optional prayer

Actions shout louder than words. Help us, God, to match what we say with what we do. May the messages we send about ourselves be true to what we really are.

Music suggestions

'You can't stop rain', *Junior Praise 1*, compiled by P. Horrobin and G. Leavers (Marshall Pickering, 1986).
'No one else', *Children's Praise,* compiled by P. Burt et al. (Marshall Pickering, 1991).

Assembly 12

Themes: Minds, bodies and emotions/The woman with a haemorrhage

Painting: Christ addressing a Kneeling Woman
by Paolo Veronese

You will need:
- Mixing bowl (younger pupils)
- Ingredients for a human being – see below (younger pupils)
- Enlarged copy of Frankenstein's monster [**O** S12a] (older pupils)
- Enlarged illustration of body chemicals [**O** S12b] (optional)
- Paper and pens
- Image of **Christ addressing a Kneeling Woman** [**O** P11/12]

Introduction

> **Younger pupils**
> *Hold up a mixing bowl and tell pupils you are going to give them a recipe for a human being.* To make a human, you would need, at least, the following ingredients:
>
> Carbon *(add pencils to the bowl)*
> Water *(add water)*
> Minerals, such as iron and phosphorus *(add nails and matches)*
> Chemicals, such as chlorine *(add green-tinted water)*
> Fat *(add lard or butter)*
>
> These, however, are only a few of the basic ingredients for a body. People are much more than bodies, they also have minds, emotions and personalities.
>
> **Older pupils**
> In the 'Frankenstein' story, Dr Frankenstein wanted to make a human being. He took various ready-made ingredients – the head of one person, the body of another – and sewed them together. *(Show Frankenstein's monster.)*
>
> *Add the activity for younger pupils here.* These are just a few of the ingredients needed to make a human being. Even if we had all of the ingredients it would still only be the recipe for a human body.

Core material

Show the painting and read the biblical material. This painting by Veronese is about the way in which Jesus treated someone as a whole person, not just a body. The woman kneeling in this painting had been ill for twelve years. Not only could the doctors not help, they had made things worse, and, as medicines and doctors were not free, the woman had spent all her money. The woman was also lonely because other people avoided her, as the man in white at the front of the painting does. He even holds his clothes away from her so that she does not touch him. The Bible says that she crept up to Jesus and touched his cloak, believing he could cure her. She did not ask openly to be cured as she had suffered years of rejection and did not want to risk rejection again. She was desperately concerned not to draw attention to herself.

The artist has put the woman in the centre of the painting, which represents the moment when she reluctantly came forward and knelt at Jesus' feet. It almost seems cruel of Jesus to draw attention to her in this way and make her kneel there in the middle of a crowd, but he knew the cure was not finished. She might be cured of her illness, but she had suffered emotionally, too, so her emotions and relationships needed healing as well. For twelve years, people had avoided her. He wanted to show everyone that she was cured so that people would mix with her again.

Other people would have avoided the touch of this woman because of her disease. Jesus welcomes her touch and draws attention to it. He also corrects any misunderstanding she had about her healing. He did not want her to think it was magic. Christians call Jesus 'the healer', but they believe he healed more than hurt bodies: they believe he healed hurt minds, relationships, emotions and spirits as well. It is not enough to heal someone's body; often their feelings need healing as well.

Something to think about

Sometimes we have check-ups to make sure we are healthy. We are encouraged to eat healthily and take exercise to say fit. We also need to make sure our emotions and minds stay healthy. We need to check the diet we feed our minds, and check up on how we are feeling and how we are relating to other people. A spiritual check-up is as important as a health check-up.

Optional prayer

Minds, bodies, spirits and feelings – you made us whole, Lord.
Mind, bodies, spirits and feelings – you made us complex, Lord.
When one part goes wrong, the others are affected. Help us to look after our whole selves, in order to enjoy the world you gave us, and better serve you and others.

Music suggestions

'Don't hang around on the edge', *Wake Up, World!,* compiled by M. Forster and C. Tambling (Kevin Mayhew, 1993).
'Put your hand in the hand of the man from Galilee', *Alleluya!,* compiled by D. Gadsby and J. Hogarth (A. & C. Black, 1980).

Christ blessing the Children

by Nicolaes Maes (1634–1693)

Background to the painting

Date: 1652–3

Medium: oil on canvas

Dimensions: 206 cm x 154 cm

Nicolaes Maes (*Nikolass Mah-ss*) was born in Dordrecht, the son of a prosperous merchant. He became a pupil of Rembrandt in c.1650 but left his tutor's studio by 1653. This subject was portrayed by Rembrandt and by a number of his pupils, including Maes. This picture was originally thought to be by Rembrandt but now it is generally agreed that it is an early painting of Maes. It probably dates from his time in Rembrandt's studio, or just after he left it.

In this early painting, the colours reflect the black, browns and reds used by Rembrandt as well as the latter's use of light. The figure on the extreme left may be a self-portrait by Maes. The scribbles on the slate carried by the girl cannot be read. This painting is life-size, the only one which Maes ever did on such a scale. Maes often painted ordinary women and children going about everyday tasks and gave them dignity. The people are dressed in ordinary Dutch seventeenth-century clothes but Jesus is in a timeless 'biblical' robe and is barefoot. This distinction is made to underline the timelessness of Jesus for Christians. He is a man for all people of all times. In the mid 1650s, Maes was ranked among the most innovative Dutch artists, owing to his skill for portraying expressive poses, gestures and faces.

Biblical material

Mark 10:13–16 – Blessing the Children

Some parents brought their children to Jesus, hoping he would place his hands on them and bless them. When his disciples saw them coming they told the people to go away and to stop bothering Jesus. When Jesus saw the disciples doing this he became angry and said, 'Let the children come to me. Don't try to stop them. People who are like these little children belong to God's Kingdom. You should learn from the way these children respond to God.' Then Jesus took the children in his arms, placed his hands on each one and blessed them.

Assembly 13

Themes: Values and attitudes/Jesus' response to children

 ## Painting: Christ blessing the Children
by Nicolaes Maes

You will need:
- A desk and chair, a diary, a mobile phone (for drama option)
- Enlarged copy of 'The Rights of the Child' [○ S13]
- Image of **Christ blessing the Children [○ P13/14]**

Note: This assembly could be used on Children in Need Day/Universal Child Rights Day (November 20th).

Introduction

Drama option
One person sits at a desk with a phone and a diary. The telephone keeps ringing and each time the person calling asks for an appointment to see the manager. The secretary should turn down the first two callers, saying that the manager is busy or in a meeting. The third caller is important and is immediately given an appointment.

Alternative
Talk about what makes people important in other people's eyes. Examples:

*Position: Headteacher, Prime Minister, the Queen
Fame: filmstar, singer, sportsperson
Clothes they wear: designer label, expensive clothes
Looks: fitting the image of the day*

Some people respond to how important a person is, not to the person themselves; this shows what they value. The first two callers in the sketch might have had important needs, but because they were ordinary people the secretary refused them an interview.

Core material

Show the painting. In this painting, by Nicolaes Maes, we see a tired-looking Jesus blessing a shy, bewildered toddler with her finger in her mouth. Her mother pushes her forward with one hand, while grandmother looks with disapproval at the father who has tried to jump the queue by lifting his baby over the heads of the people. *Read the biblical material.*

In first-century Jewish society, children were valued, particularly boys. Despite this, children were of low status and so the disciples turned them away. Jesus was angry and told the disciples to let the children come to him. He spent time with children when he was tired. By doing this, he showed that his view of status was different from the views of the rest of society. His values were different. The artist has stressed this by showing Jesus holding a girl rather than a boy.

There are different ways in which we can detect a person's values and attitudes. Here are some of the points we can use to judge a person's values. *Ask pupils which ones they think are accurate.*

What people give time and energy to
What people give money to
How they respond to other people

Jesus had little money, so we can forget that one. But he did give time and energy to these children. Christians believe that his behaviour showed his values. Children have rights in our society. The United Nations even list the rights of children in a charter. *(Display the list.)* But words alone, even written words, are not enough. Values have to be expressed in time, words, money and behaviour.

Something to think about

Values are invisible things but we all have them. Imagine a Martian coming to earth and watching you for a day. If the visitor watched what you did and how you spent your time and money, would he or she get a good picture of your values?

Optional prayer

Thank you, God, for the example of Jesus, who was prepared to spend time with children, even though others thought they were not important. Help us to show what we think is important by the way we spend our time and money and the way we respond to people.

Music suggestions

'Who took fish and bread?', *Junior Praise 1*, compiled by P. Horrobin and G. Leavers (Marshall Pickering, 1986).
'Jesus had all kinds of friends', *Wake Up, World!*, compiled by M. Forster and C. Tambling (Kevin Mayhew, 1993).

Assembly 14

Theme: Realizing the significance of important moments

Painting: Christ blessing the Children
by Nicolaes Maes

You will need:
- A camera, two dolls, a chair (for drama option)
- Enlarged copy of examples of important moments [**O** S14] (optional)
- Paper and pens
- Image of **Christ blessing the Children [O P13/14]**

Introduction

Before the assembly arrange for several pupils to ask members of staff about an important moment in their lives that they would be happy to share.

Younger pupils
During the assembly pupils can report back on the responses of members of staff.

Older pupils
Staff can be interviewed during the assembly.

Alternative
Use the examples provided.

Core material

Show the painting.

Drama option
One person can act as photographer and create the following scene: arrange a group of pupils as in the painting. You will not need all the figures. You will need the two women and the young child, and the father at the back. You will also need two dolls: one doll to act as the child that the father lifts up, and another to act as the baby on the woman's hip. The photographer gets them into place and takes a photograph. As soon as this has been done, the people whose picture has just been taken improvise what they think the characters are saying. This creates a sound commentary on the painting. For example, the grandmother might be moaning at the father for trying to jump the queue.

Alternative
Talk about important people you, or they, would like to meet or hold a telephone conversation with. Why would they like to meet/talk to these people?

The little girl in this painting by Nicolaes Maes looks as if she would much rather be off playing elsewhere, or perhaps at school, for she has her slate with her. Maybe she would rather be eating the apple which she holds tightly in her hand. She looks shy and bewildered, and Jesus holds on to her arm almost as if she will wander off if he lets go. Her mother pushes her forward. If we were to add a speech bubble to this painting the girl might be saying something like: 'I want to play' or 'Where's my mother?' or 'I want to eat my apple'. *These words can be written up.* If we could add a speech bubble for the mother, it might read: 'You can play later. It won't take long.' The painting shows us a moment when Jesus welcomed children. *Read the biblical material.*

The little girl does not know the significance of the moment, but her mum does. Often we look back on life and realize that what we thought at the time were just ordinary events were in fact very important ones. If you go to Coventry Cathedral and stand at the back of the cathedral, facing the altar, you see nothing but plain stone walls on either side. If you walk to the altar and look back, those side walls are full of colour. Stained glass windows have been placed all along the walls, but at an angle, so that you can only see them once you have walked past them. Life is often like that. We get on with everyday living. Only when we look back do we realize that events that seemed ordinary at the time were actually important moments.

Something to think about

Think back over the last year. Run it like a video through your mind. What was an important moment for you? Did you appreciate that it was an important moment at the time?

Optional prayer

For the moments whose importance we missed,
Forgive us, Lord.
For the important times that passed us by,
Forgive us, Lord.
As we look back on life, help us to sort out the events that were really important,
and give each one an important place in our memories.

Music suggestions

'Jesus' hands were kind hands' and 'God knows my name', *Children's Praise*, compiled by G. Leavers and P. Burt (Marshall Pickering, 1991).

Christ washing his Disciples' Feet

by Jacopo Tintoretto (1518–1594)

Background to the painting

Date: about 1556

Medium: oil (identified) on canvas

Dimensions: 200.6 cm x 408.3 cm

Tintoretto's real family name was Robusti. His nickname 'Tintoretto' *(Yah-ko-poh Tin-torr-etto)* came from his father's profession of dyer (tintore). Most of Tintoretto's life was spent in Venice, where, with Veronese and Titian, he was a leading artist. He was a devout man and was famous for his large dramatic religious paintings. To help him with the poses of the people in his paintings, Tintoretto experimented with lighting, using wax models which he arranged on a small stage. Two of Tintoretto's sons and his daughter, Maria, also helped in his studio.

This painting captures the moment when Peter protests about Jesus washing his feet. It came from a chapel in Venice. A replica of this painting now replaces it and hangs opposite Tintoretto's **Last Supper** – an appropriate subject for a chapel dedicated to the Sacrament.

Biblical material

John 13:1–17

It was almost time for the Passover and Jesus knew that it was time for him to die. He also knew that Judas, one of his disciples, would betray him. Jesus was concerned for his followers. During the meal he got up, took off his outer tunic and wrapped a towel round his waist. He put some water into a bowl and began washing his disciples' feet and drying them on the towel he was wearing.

Simon Peter protested. 'Lord! You're not going to wash my feet!'

Jesus answered, 'You don't understand what I am doing now but you will understand later.'

'You'll never wash my feet!' Peter replied.

'If I don't, you don't really belong to me,' said Jesus.

'Then wash my hands and my head as well!' responded Peter.

'No need,' replied Jesus. 'Your feet are enough.'

After Jesus had washed his disciples' feet he put on his tunic and sat down. 'Do you understand what I have done?' he said. 'You call me your teacher and leader, which is quite right because that is what I am. I'm also your Lord. If I, your Lord and teacher, can wash your feet, you should be able to do this for each other. I have set you an example which you should follow.'

Assembly 15

Themes: Authority and power/Power to serve

Painting: Christ washing his Disciples' Feet

by Jacopo Tintoretto

You will need:
- Copy printed on paper of examples of jobs and powers [**O** S15a], cut up
- Copy printed on paper of corresponding responsibilities [**O** S15b], cut up
- Image of **Christ washing his Disciples' Feet** [**O** P15/16]

Introduction

> **Younger pupils**
> *Use two or three of the examples of jobs, powers and responsibilities.*
>
> **Older pupils**
> *Use all of the examples.*

Either use the copies you have prepared or write each item on a separate piece of paper. Give the jobs and powers papers to eight pupils. Ask the pupils to read their papers and then get themselves into pairs. Each pair should consist of the title of a person and the type of action they have the authority or power to carry out. For example: President/The power to declare war. Finally, hand out the responsibilities papers to another four pupils and ask them to stand by the people they think have this responsibility or opportunity. Talk about the responsibility that power brings.

Core material

Show the painting. Read the biblical material. In this painting by Jacopo Tintoretto, we see Jesus washing the disciples' feet. This would be an unpleasant job at the best of times, and even more unpleasant in a hot country where people wore sandals. Not even slaves could be made to wash feet! A slave was a person with no authority at all, yet Jesus did the job that was beneath a slave. That is why we see Peter protesting in this painting. Look at his body language: he leans forward and throws out his arms.

We see Jesus' disciples at their last meeting with Jesus before his death. Jesus, surrounded by light, is in the centre of the painting. His face is that of a young man; he was only in his thirties. The disciples are scattered about the room, some drying their feet, others sitting on benches. Jesus had been teaching his disciples for about three years, but they were slow to understand some things. The disciples had seen Jesus act with great power, they had heard him teach with great authority, but still they did not realize that Jesus' understanding of the words 'power' and 'authority' was different from everyone else's. Peter's reaction shows how puzzled they were.

For the rest of the world, having power and authority meant being able to boss other people about. But Jesus showed by his behaviour that authority and power meant having the opportunity to serve others. *(Refer back to the introduction and the last four cards in particular.)* Just before his death, Jesus tried to demonstrate this teaching by washing his disciples' feet – he is shown here with a towel and a basin. If he was to leave them, they must understand that leadership, authority and power mean responsibility and the opportunity to serve, not just the right to tell other people what to do.

It is a difficult idea. Two thousand years later, Jesus' ideas about authority and power are as radical as they were in the first century. Some people still think having power is just for their own benefit. They think it gives them the right to boss others around and get their own way. They don't realize that it can mean they have the opportunity to serve others.

Something to think about

Think about the news you hear on the radio and television. Think about one piece of news that would change if people saw power as an opportunity for service rather than being for their personal benefit.

Optional prayer

Power, in one form or another, comes to us all at some time. One day we will be in a position to influence others. We may even have the power to change other people's lives. Give us the strength, Lord, to resist the temptations of power. Help us to use our power to serve.

Music suggestions

'From Heaven you came', *A Year of Celebration*, by J. Porter and J. MacCrimmon (MacCrimmon).
'Make me a servant', *Junior Praise 1*, compiled by P. Horrobin and G. Leavers (Marshall Pickering, 1986).

Assembly 16

Themes: Saying goodbye/Leaving a lasting legacy

Painting: Christ washing his Disciples' Feet
by Jacopo Tintoretto

You will need:
- A DVD player, TV and suitable DVD – see below (for DVD option)
- Image of **Christ washing his Disciples' Feet** [**O** P15/16]

Introduction

DVD option

> **Older pupils**
> *Show a DVD clip suitable for the age group. Choose a scene where people say goodbye and spend some time with their friends before they leave.*

Alternative follow-up for DVD clip
The teacher can write a list of what pupils might do on their last evening with a friend who was moving from the area (e.g. go for a pizza, watch a film). Comment on each activity.

> **Younger pupils**
> *Ask what they would do on their last evening if a friend was moving away from the area.*

Last moments are precious. When our friends are leaving school or moving we want to spend time with them. To waste that time would be something we would regret.

Core material

Show the painting and read the biblical material.
In this painting by Jacopo Tintoretto we see Jesus' last evening with his friends. The first thing he did was to eat a final meal with them: that is a common way of saying goodbye. As part of that meal, they had shared bread and wine together. At the end of the meal, he told them to continue to share bread and wine together in order to remember him. Jesus left them with something very practical as a reminder of the friendship. Christians still do this: it is called Communion, Eucharist or the Lord's Supper. To be given a practical memento of a friend is not a waste of time. Think about friends who have left. Do you have ways of remembering them?

The next thing Jesus did was to wash his disciples' feet, and this is what the artist depicts in the painting. We can see Jesus with a towel around his waist and a bowl of water. He is on his knees in front of his disciples: this is not a position of authority. Jesus did the very worst job for them – foot washing. Not even a slave could be compelled to wash someone's feet. That is why Peter looks shocked and protests. Given that time was short, was this a waste of time? The answer lies in the colour of the painting.

This painting is very dark. Tintoretto did this deliberately by painting over a dark bottom layer. It represents a very 'dark' episode in Jesus' life. Not only was Jesus about to die, he was about to be betrayed by one of his own disciples – Judas. Judas may be the figure carrying the torch on the left. He is just about to leave to betray Jesus to his enemies. These two events could have broken up the band of disciples, for Judas' betrayal shook them and Jesus' death shattered them and left them leaderless.

The Bible story makes it clear that Jesus was aware of what his disciples were about to face. His actions on that last evening did not happen by chance: they were meant to help the disciples stay together after his death. When Jesus washed their feet he gave the disciples a new way of looking at power and authority. Power became the opportunity to serve. This changed their attitude towards each other.

After the crucifixion, the disciples did not fight over who was to be the new leader. The group was not destroyed by power struggles. Far from being a waste of time, Jesus' actions were very practical, for he gave his disciples a lasting legacy or gift when he gave them a new way of thinking about power. We tend to think that in the tough 'real' world only ambition, power and ruthlessness count. We may think that things like caring and humility are only for family and close friends. But Jesus' action demonstrated that these qualities can sometimes be good politics, as well as being good in themselves.

Something to think about

Jesus left his disciples a lasting gift in the way he changed their thinking. When friends say goodbye, they sometimes leave something behind in the memories we have of them and the way they changed us. Think of a friend who you no longer see. What difference did they make to your life?

Optional prayer

Thank you, God, for the memories we treasure. Thank you for the people who we no longer see but who are part of us. Help us to build good memories for others, and leave a legacy of love.

Music suggestions

'Let us break bread together', *Mango Spice*, compiled by Y. Connolly et al. (A. & C. Black, 1981).
'Jesus put a song into our hearts', *A Year of Celebration*, by J. Porter and J. MacCrimmon (MacCrimmon).

The Betrayal of Christ

by Ugolino di Nerio (active 1317–1327)

Background to the painting

Date: about 1324–5

Medium: tempera on poplar

Dimensions: 40.5 cm x 58.5 cm

This panel was originally part of an altarpiece in the church of Santa Croce, Florence. It showed scenes from Jesus' passion (death and resurrection). The altarpiece remained complete until the late eighteenth century, when an inscription beneath the central panel was recorded: *Ugolino of Siena painted me.* Ugolino di Nerio *(Oogoh-leenoh dee Nair-ee-oh)* was possibly a pupil of Duccio. He took his ideas for the sequence of paintings, of which this painting forms a part, from Duccio's altarpiece (page 9). He simplified Duccio's scenes and made them more dramatic, as in this scene of the betrayal. He painted many pictures and chapels in all parts of Italy but only the altarpiece referred to bears his signature. At the centre of this painting, Judas betrays Jesus. On the left, Saint Peter cuts off the ear of Malchus, a servant of the High Priest. Only Jesus and Peter are depicted with haloes.

Biblical material

Matthew 26:14–16, 20–25, 36–56

Judas Iscariot was one of Jesus' twelve disciples. He went to the religious leaders and asked them how much they would give him if he helped them to trap Jesus. The leaders paid Judas thirty pieces of silver and from that moment on Judas looked for a good chance to betray Jesus.

Later that evening, when Jesus was eating a meal with his disciples, he told them that one of them would betray him to his enemies. The disciples were upset and looked at each other and said, 'You can't mean me?' Jesus replied, 'Someone who's shared the same dish of food with me will betray me. But I pity the man who does it.' Judas said, 'Teacher, surely you don't mean me?' 'The words are yours,' Jesus replied. But later Judas did betray him.

After the meal Jesus and his disciples went to pray in a quiet place called Gethsemane. He took Peter, James and John to a quiet corner of the garden. There he went a little distance from them in order to pray by himself. While Jesus prayed alone the three disciples slept. Jesus prayed to his father. 'My father, if there is any other way, take this cup of suffering from me. But I will do whatever needs to be done.' Jesus came back and woke up the disciples. 'Are you still sleeping? Couldn't you stay awake just a little while? Never mind. The time has come for me to be handed over to my enemies. Get up. Let's go. My betrayer is coming.'

While he was still speaking, Judas arrived with a large mob armed with swords and clubs. They had been sent by the nation's leaders. Judas had given them a signal, 'The one I greet with a kiss is Jesus. Arrest him.' Judas walked right up to Jesus and greeted him with the words, 'Peace be with you, teacher,' and kissed him. Jesus replied, 'My friend, why have you come?' The men grabbed Jesus and arrested him. But Peter pulled out a sword and cut off the ear of one of the crowd. Jesus told him to put away his sword. 'Those who live by the sword die by it,' said Jesus. 'Don't you know my father could rescue me at any moment if only I gave the word?' He turned to the crowd. 'Why do you come here with swords and clubs to arrest me like a common criminal? Daily I taught in the temple and you could have arrested me at any moment. Never mind, all this is coming true just as the scriptures said it would.' And all of Jesus' disciples left him and ran away.

Assembly 17

Themes: Friendship/Betrayal

Painting: The Betrayal of Christ

by Ugolino di Nerio

You will need:

- A ball of wool or string and a pair of scissors (younger pupils)
- Enlarged copy of the relationships web [**O** S17a]
- Enlarged copy of the Jesus and his friends web [**O** S17b]
- Image of **The Betrayal of Christ** [**O** P17/18]

Introduction

Younger pupils
Arrange a few pupils in a circle. Holding on to one end of a ball of wool, the first person throws/passes the ball to another pupil (not the one next to her). That pupil holds on to the wool but throws/passes the ball to another pupil. Carry on until a 'web' is formed. One person produces a pair of scissors and cuts their particular loop and the rest pull and the whole thing comes undone. Talk about the way the actions of one person can wreck a whole group of friends.

Older pupils
Any group of friends makes quite a complex web. *Use the relationships web. Draw coloured lines to show friendships within the group. Emma gets on well with Amy. Shanta and Miriam are best friends. And so on.* But there are lots of things that can destroy the web of friendship, such as one person spreading gossip, bullying, and so on.

Core material

Show the painting. In this painting by Ugolino de Nerio, we see Jesus with his group of disciples. They are the grey-haired men dressed in green. They had been together for three years. Together they had walked the hills of Galilee. They had been hungry and tired together, they had laughed and eaten together. Those three years had welded them together as a group.

Use the Jesus and his friends web. Everyone related to Jesus. There were, however, other lines of friendship within the group: James, John and Peter were friends; Philip and Nathaniel were friends. One thing that dramatically changed the pattern of friendship of Jesus' disciples was the death of Jesus. *(Cross out Jesus.)* Another was the betrayal of Jesus by Judas. *(Cross out Judas.)* Once that happened, the lines had to be radically redrawn.

Read the biblical material. When Judas cut the web of friendship by betraying Jesus to his enemies, the whole group fell apart. The Bible says that they all ran away as soon as danger threatened. Here we see some of them just before they run away. Judas is shown at the front of the painting, greeting Jesus with a kiss (the greeting used by friends). That greeting is like the cut of the scissors: it is the moment when the web of friendship, built up over three years, is cut. Judas had offered to betray Jesus for thirty pieces of silver, the price of an average slave. Why did he do it? It couldn't have been just for money, for the price on Jesus' head must have been much more than the price of an average slave. The authorities were desperate to get rid of him: Judas could have asked for more.

Judas had stuck by Jesus for three years. Maybe he had put all his hopes in him, but then found that Jesus was not the sort of person he wanted him to be. Maybe he betrayed Jesus out of disappointment. Judas may have had his own ideas of what a Messiah (a special king) should be. Perhaps he really wanted a superman – the sort who would turn into a superhero and defeat the enemy. Instead, Jesus was the sort of hero who forgave his enemies and tried to change them.

Whatever his motive, Judas broke the web of friendship. Imagine the impact on the disciples: first they lose Jesus, then they find out that one of their own group betrayed him – someone with whom they had lived for three years.

Something to think about

Judas destroyed a good friendship and we will never really know his motives. There are times when friendships go wrong and the friendship has to be broken. There are times when the web has to be cut if friends are pushing us into the wrong type of behaviour, but Judas had none of these excuses. We need to know when to protect a relationship and when to cut the web.

Optional prayer

Friendship makes life worthwhile.
Help us to protect it, Lord.
Friendship sometimes goes wrong.
Give us the wisdom to know when to cut the thread.

Music suggestions

'Jesus in the garden', *The Complete Come and Praise*, compiled by G. Marshall-Taylor (BBC, 1990).
'Bind us together', *Junior Praise 1*, compiled by P. Horrobin and G. Leavers (Marshall Pickering, 1986).

Assembly 18

Themes: The ups and downs of life/Life as a cup

 Painting: The Betrayal of Christ
by Ugolino di Nerio

You will need:

- Enlarged copy of the word-pictures illustrations [**O** S18a]
- Two enlarged copies of the cup [**O** S18b]
- Large felt-tip for drawing on one of the cups
- Image of **The Betrayal of Christ** [**O** P17/18]

Introduction

> **Younger pupils**
> *Select from the illustrations and ask pupils to say what they have in common.*
>
> **Older pupils**
> *Use all the illustrations and explain or ask pupils what they have in common.*
>
> A roller coaster ride (has ups and downs)
> A journey (with its hills and valleys)
> A lift (goes up and down)
> A song (with high and low notes)

These are all different metaphors (word-pictures) for life. They all have one thing in common – highs and lows. *Talk about what might be a 'high' and what might be a 'low' in life .*

Core material

Show the painting. This painting by Ugolino de Nerio is about a low spot, one of the lowest points in Jesus' life: the moment when one of his friends betrayed him. *Read the biblical material.*

The night before he died, Jesus went to a garden to pray quietly. The garden is represented in the painting by just three trees. Jesus took three of his disciples to a distant part of the garden. These disciples – Peter, James and John – are seen in green with grey hair. He then left the three disciples and went to pray by himself. He prayed that there might be some other way, besides a cross.

In his prayer, Jesus described what he was about to face as a 'cup of suffering' that he would drink if there was no other alternative. In the Bible, life is often described as a cup. Sometimes it is full to overflowing with good things – like a sweet drink. At other times it is full of suffering – like a bitter drink. Life is likened to a cup, but the drink that fills the cup is sometimes sweet and sometimes bitter. It's like the word-pictures in the introduction that described the ups and downs of life. Life is not all ups, neither is it all downs. It is not all sweet, neither is it all bitter. There had been good times for Jesus and his disciples, but now was not one of them. The moment the artist has captured is when Jesus' life was full of bitter suffering.

In this painting we see three things which added to the 'cup of suffering'. *Use one copy of the cup. Add a strip of colour to the cup, using a large felt-pen, as each of the sections below are read. The cup should progessively 'fill' with colour.*

(1) Judas greets Jesus with a kiss as a signal to the soldiers. We see this at the front of the painting. The kiss was the normal way for friends to greet each other. Jesus' own friend betrayed him.

(2) On the left, Peter cuts off the ear of one the people who had come to arrest Jesus. Peter knew only one way of dealing with trouble and that was to hit back. Jesus stopped him, with the words 'Those who live by the sword, die by the sword'. It must have been depressing for Jesus: Peter had been with him for three years and still he did not understand that Jesus did not use violence.

(3) Finally, the soldiers, shown on the right, arrest him. We see them in armour and carrying spears and torches. They treated Jesus like a common criminal although he had done nothing wrong.

This was only the beginning. There was more to come.

Something to think about

Show the second cup. Think about your life at the moment. How would you describe your cup of life? One temptation is to expect life's cup to be sweet all the time, to expect things to go well always. Another temptation is to expect things to go wrong all the time and expect the cup always to be bitter. Life is a mixture of both. If we expect things always to go well, we will be disappointed. If we always expect things to go wrong, we will miss out on a lot.

Optional prayer

When our cup is full of happiness,
Help us to share it, Lord.
When our cup is full of sadness,
Give us the courage to ask for help to face it.

Music suggestions

'When I'm feeling down and sad', *Big Blue Planet,* edited by J. Jarvis (Stainer & Bell and Methodist Church Division of Education and Youth, 1995). 'Father, I place into your hands', *Junior Praise 1,* compiled by P. Horrobin and G. Leavers (Marshall Pickering, 1986).

Christ carrying his Cross

by Giampietrino (active 1500–1550)

Background to the painting

Date: probably about 1510–30

Medium: oil on poplar

Dimensions: painted surface 59.7 cm x 47 cm

Giampietrino (*Jam-pet-rreeno*) was also known as Giovanni Pedrino or Rizzoli. In this painting of Jesus carrying his cross to Golgotha, Jesus turns his head to look out of the picture but we do not see what he glances at. This painting may be based on a design by Leonardo da Vinci, who greatly influenced Giampietrino and other artists working in Milan in the first half of the sixteenth century. Giampietrino painted intense luminous colours of draperies, often in contrast to dark backgrounds, as in this painting. Some of Giampietrino's paintings are characterized by a small white vase which may be his symbolic signature.

Biblical material

Luke 23:26–43

Jesus was led away to his death by soldiers. These same soldiers seized hold of a man from Cyrene called Simon. They put Jesus' cross on him and made him carry it behind Jesus. A large crowd was following Jesus and there were a lot of women who were crying and weeping. But Jesus turned and comforted them and said, 'Don't cry for me. Weep for yourselves for bad times are coming.'

Two criminals were put to death with Jesus. When the soldiers came to a place known as 'The Skull' they nailed Jesus to a cross. The two criminals were also nailed to crosses and placed on either side of Jesus.

Jesus said, 'Father, forgive them, they don't know what they're doing.'

The crowds stood there watching Jesus die and soldiers gambled for his clothes. The leaders mocked him, saying, 'He saved others, now he should save himself if he really is a king.'

The soldiers too made fun of Jesus. 'If you're King of the Jews, save yourself,' they said.

Above him was a sign and on it were written the words: 'This is the King of the Jews'. One of the criminals hanging there also jeered at Jesus, saying, 'Well, aren't you the King? Save yourself and us.'

But the other criminal told him off, saying, 'Don't you fear God? We got what we deserved but he hasn't done anything wrong.' Then he turned to Jesus and said, 'Remember me when you come as a king.' Jesus replied, 'Today you will be with me in Paradise.'

Assembly 19

Themes: When it is hard to care/The women and a stranger at the cross

Painting: Christ carrying his Cross
by Giampietrino

You will need:
- Wallpaper and pens or enlarged copy of the outline of a person [**O** S19]
- Blu-Tack
- The poem 'The Whether Outlook' on page 45
- Image of **Christ carrying his Cross** [**O** P19/20]

Introduction

> **Younger pupils**
> *Ask someone to lie down on the wallpaper, with their feet together. Draw round them. Label the resulting outline 'Chris'. Ask pupils to imagine that Chris's friend is in trouble. Will Chris help? Using pupil suggestions, write around and inside the figure the reasons why he/she may, or may not, help his/her friend. Some reasons come from the inside: for example, not caring, laziness. Others are based on outside things, such as lack of time and what other people think.*
>
> **Older pupils**
> *Use the outline of a person. Do the same activity as above. Explain why it may be difficult to help in some circumstances: for example, it may depend on how popular the person is.*

Core material

Show the painting. In this painting by Giampietrino, someone, or several people, are missing. Jesus turns his head and looks out of the painting. His cross points forward but he looks backwards; who is he looking at? It is someone we cannot see, or it may be a group of people. The answer probably lies in Luke's Gospel. *Read the biblical material.*

Jesus may be looking at the group of women who were following. Amongst this group of women were probably his mother and some of his female disciples. Jesus had always had women disciples. They included Joanna, Mary Magdalene and Susanna. There were many others who had either followed him during his three years of teaching, or, like Mary and Martha, had offered him a temporary home when he needed it.

The Bible records that most of Jesus' male disciples ran away when he was arrested, but the women stuck with him to the end. The women followed him to the cross, and they were there at the resurrection. Only one of the male disciples is recorded as being present at the crucifixion, and that is John.

There is one other person who is missing from this painting – a man from Libya in North Africa called Simon. When Jesus, weak from the beating, could carry his cross no longer, Simon carried it for him. Simon may have been a visitor to Jerusalem, just there for the festival of Passover. Maybe it is Simon who Jesus glances at in this painting. When Jesus was really in need of help, he was supported by women and a stranger.

It is easy to care when things are going well, but when you are frightened, tired or bored it is a different matter. Some people will only care if they can see something in it for themselves. (*Older pupils:* The extremes of this attitude are reflected in the poem 'The Whether Outlook' by Gordon Bailey. *Read the poem.*) The women in this story faced danger by following Jesus to the cross. It allowed people to identify them as his friends.

Something to think about

How far would you put yourself out for a friend? What sometimes stops you helping? Is it boredom, lack of time, lack of care, what other people think? *Read the poem again if you choose.*

Optional prayer

Lord, teach us to be friends when it matters:
When other people desert,
When others fail to care,
When it is unfashionable to love.
Teach us to care when it matters.

Music suggestions

'When I survey' and 'There is a green hill', *Junior Praise 1*, compiled by P. Horrobin and G. Leavers (Marshall Pickering, 1986).

Assembly 20

Themes: Different types of love/The cross as a symbol of love

Painting: Christ carrying his Cross
by Giampietrino

You will need:
- Either enlarged printed copies of the cross and heart [**O** S20a,b] or your own drawings. The heart should be cut out.
- Paper and pens (optional)
- Cross jewellery (optional)
- Image of **Christ carrying his Cross [O P19/20]**

Introduction

Some words have changed in meaning over a period of time.

> **Younger pupils**
> *Select only a few words from the list.*
>
> **Older pupils**
> *Use all the examples.*

In 1500, 'naughty' could mean serious crime punishable by death.
Today, 'naughty' is a word used of little children.
In 1920, 'cool' meant slightly cold.
By 1960, it meant fashionable.
In 1930, 'wicked' meant evil.
In 1980, it meant good.
In 1940, 'hardware' was nails and metal objects.
Today, 'hardware' means computers.

Drama option
Show how confusion can occur across the generations by using some of the words above in short sketches.

Alternative
Put the words in sentences to show their meaning or to show how their meaning could be misunderstood by different generations.

Symbols as well as words can change in meaning. The cross was once a symbol of death. For Christians, it is now a symbol of love.

Core material

Sometimes, people are criticized for wearing a cross symbol as a necklace. Some people think it is inappropriate, as the cross was once a way of killing people. The cross has completely changed its meaning over 2000 years. *(Show the cross or draw a cross on paper.)* The cross today is a Christian symbol for love and is similar to wearing a heart-shaped symbol. *(Show the heart symbol or draw a heart.)* How did the cross change its meaning from death to love?

Show the painting. Once the cross stood only for pain and suffering. In this painting by Giampietrino, we see Jesus carrying the cross. (He later staggered under its weight, and Simon of Cyrene carried it for him.) Jesus looks back but he is prepared to go on: the cross points forward. It is that glance and that determination to carry on that are the key. In this painting, Jesus is shown on his way to die. *Read the biblical material.*

Christians believe that Jesus' death turned the cross from a symbol of pain and suffering to a symbol of love, because they believe love was his motive. As a result, the cross is now a symbol of love. Many people wear it as a necklace. For some people, it is like wearing a heart symbol. There are, however, differences between the cross and the heart symbol. Both symbolize love, but the word 'love' can mean many things in English. We say:

I love chips.
I love my dog.
I love my mum.
I love my boyfriend or girlfriend. *(Older pupils)*

In each case, we mean something slightly different. *Write up the sentences and ask pupils to suggest words that will replace love in each case.* We only have one word for love. In Jesus' time there were four words. The word 'love' used of God's love in the Bible is the word *agape* (pronounced *agapay*). It means a love which gives to others. It is a selfless love. The cross stands for *agape*. The heart symbol is a different type of love: it concentrates on feelings.

Something to think about

Show the cross. Place or redraw the heart over the centre of the cross. Often when we use the word 'love', we concentrate on what we feel. The cross is a reminder that love can be about what we can give to others, even if we don't feel like it.

Optional prayer

Often we focus on ourselves: how we feel, the impact of events on us. The cross is a reminder of a love that concentrates on others: how they feel, the impact of events on them. Help us, Lord, to grow in this kind of love.

Music suggestions

'When I think about the cross', *Songs for Every Easter,* by M. and H. Johnson (Out of the Ark Music, 1996).
'Two long pieces of wood', *Big Blue Planet,* edited by J. Jarvis (Stainer & Bell and Methodist Church Division of Education and Youth, 1995).

Christ rising from the Tomb

by Ferrari Gaudenzio (1475–1546)

Background to the painting

Date: 1530–46

Medium: oil on poplar

Dimensions: 152.4 cm x 84.5 cm

Ferrari Gaudenzio *(Ferr-ah-rree Gow-dent-zee-oh)* was a painter and sculptor who worked in a number of Italian cities, but his main success was achieved in the city of Vercelli. His work was often realistic in detail and portrayed emotion with intensity through rich and expressive colour. In later works, he expressed emotion more through theatrical language of gesture and expression.

In this painting, Jesus rises from the tomb, triumphant over death. One hand holds a banner, the other is raised in blessing. This may have been the centre panel of an altarpiece from the church of San Pietro at Maggianico, near Lecco. The size of the panels and the scale of the figures suggest this.

Biblical material

Luke 24:1–9

Early on the Sunday morning, the women went to the tomb, carrying spices to place on Jesus' body. They found that the circular stone which sealed the tomb had been rolled away from the entrance.

They went inside but they did not find the body of Jesus and they were puzzled and did not know what to think about it. Suddenly two men in shining clothes stood by them, and the women bowed to the ground with fear. But the men said, 'Why are you looking in a tomb – the place of the dead – for someone who is alive? Jesus is not here, he has been raised from the dead.' Then the women remembered Jesus' words and went back to tell the disciples.

Assembly 21

Themes: When life defeats us/Victory over death

 Painting: Christ rising from the Tomb
by Ferrari Gaudenzio

You will need:
- Copies of the drama outlines below – see also [**O** S21]
- Some NIKE clothing
- Beethoven's Fifth Symphony on CD
- A magazine (older pupils)
- A candle and matches
- Image of **Christ rising from the Tomb** [**O** P21/22]

Introduction

The following two dramas can be improvised around the structure suggested.

Drama 1. In the Gym (All pupils)
Two people are working out. Both are wearing NIKE clothes. They comment on each other's NIKE clothes and wonder what the word means. One explains that it means 'victory' – she heard it in a history lesson.

Drama 2. Beethoven's Fifth (Older pupils)
A. Comes in, tired from school. She sits down and puts her feet up and relaxes with a magazine.
B. Enters rather hurriedly, saying she has been given free tickets for a concert. A friend bought them but he's sick and can't go.
A. Asks what type of concert the tickets are for.
B. Replies that it is Beethoven's Fifth Symphony.
A. Says she can't remember it and is not at all sure that she will like classical music.
B. Assures her that she does know it and hums/taps/plays the opening bars (da, da, da, dum …). Anyway, it's a free night out. Both exit, saying they had better get ready.

Alternatives
Show some NIKE clothing and explain what it means. Play the opening of Beethoven's Fifth Symphony and highlight the victory rhythm code (see below).

Core material

Show the painting. Read the biblical material. We are used to seeing the word NIKE on trainers and sweatshirts. It is the Greek word for victory. It is often used in pictures of Jesus because Christians believe he is a victor (winner). They believe that he defeated death at Easter by rising from the dead. The word NIKE is not used in this painting by Gaudenzio, but the painting is a picture of Jesus the victor (winner). We know this because:

(a) It is a picture of the resurrection. In the painting, Jesus steps out of the tomb with confidence, though he still bears the marks of his death. His hands and feet are scarred and there is a wound in his side.

(b) Jesus holds the victory banner. On the banner is a red cross, a symbol of the crucifixion. This is a reminder to Christians that victory was not easily won.

Explain Morse code. The Morse code for V (for victory) is dot dot dot dash. It is the same rhythm as the opening of Beethoven's Fifth Symphony. *Encourage younger pupils to tap or clap the Morse code for victory.* For Christians, it can be a reminder of the Easter victory, when love and life triumphed over hate and death. Easter is a reminder to Christians that the power of death has been broken. Death is not the end. The women arrived at the tomb mourning and defeated because Jesus was dead. They left victorious.

There are times when we all feel defeated. Life throws things at us and it is easy to become cynical.

Something to think about

Play the opening of Beethoven's Fifth Symphony and light a candle. This simple rhythm is a reminder of the Christian belief that hate and death do not have the final word. Death is still tragic and hate is still evil but they are not all-powerful. Christians believe that the candle of hope and life may be blown out (blow out the candle), but it can be relit (light it).

Optional prayer

When life seems dark,
Your resurrection is a reminder of light.
When life seems full of hate,
Your resurrection is a reminder of love.
When life seems hopeless,
Your resurrection is a reminder of life.
Lord of light, love and life,
Guide us through our lives.

Music suggestions

Play Beethoven's Fifth Symphony while pupils enter and leave.
'God's not dead', *Junior Praise 1*, compiled by P. Horrobin and G. Leavers (Marshall Pickering, 1986).
'Come and praise the Lord our King', *The Complete Come and Praise*, compiled by G. Marshall-Taylor (BBC, 1990).

Assembly 22

Themes: Love as a weapon in the battle of life/The defeat of evil

Painting: Christ rising from the Tomb
by Ferrari Gaudenzio

You will need:
- Enlarged copy of the flag [**O** S22a] or your own drawing
- Two copies of the script below for 'The Victory' – see also [**O** S22b] (for drama option)
- Image of **Christ rising from the Tomb** [**O** P21/22]

Introduction

Drama option (Older pupils)

The Victory
(The C.O. enters, shouting loudly.)
C.O. Davies! Davies! Where on earth is my communications officer? Davies!
D. Sir! *(Davies runs in and salutes.)*
C.O. Is everything secured?
D. Yes, sir. The men have just finished a final sweep through the building.
C.O. How many are wounded, Davies?
D. Over 100 sir. The medical officer and his team are with them now.
C.O. And dead?
D. 43.
C.O. I hope the world appreciates what they owe those men. Now we have captured the enemy Command Centre, they can't win. Our victory is certain. It may take a while, Davies. There will still be battles to be fought. Don't think for a moment the enemy will just give in, but we will win.
D. Yes, sir.
C.O. We had better let H.Q. know what has happened.
D. We can't, sir. The radios are out of action and the satellite link isn't up yet.
C.O. Then use old-fashioned Morse code! You were in the boy scouts, weren't you?
D. I'm not sure I can remember any Morse code, sir. It was rather a long time ago.
C.O. It's a short message, Davies, just one letter – V for Victory: dot dot dot dash. *(Taps it on wood.)*
D. Straight away, sir!
C.O. And Davies ...
D. Yes, sir?
C.O. Unfurl the flag while you're about it. We might as well let the rest of the world know we've won. *(Davies salutes and leaves, unfurling the flag on the way. The C.O. looks up at the flag, salutes and then leaves.)*

Alternative/Younger pupils
Talk about winners and losers. How is winning expressed? Examples:

Punching the air
Football chants: 'We won, we won.' 'Five nil, five nil.' 'We are the champions.'

Waving scarves/flags
Receiving medals, cups, etc.

Explain how a flag signals victory in battle. The victors unfurl their flag above a conquered city.

Core material

Show the painting and read the biblical material.
The banner in the painting by Gaudenzio, like the unfurling of the flag in the drama, is a sign of victory. Jesus steps confidently out of the tomb, one hand raised in blessing, the other carrying the victory banner. This is the scene which happened before the women arrived. When the women came to the tomb they felt defeated: it looked as if evil had won when Jesus died. But the angels (the men in shining clothes referred to in this story) announced a victory. The artist has captured this victory – Jesus rising from the tomb – in Christ's confident pose. Christians believe that the Easter victory was a triumph not only over death but also over evil.

Imagine a boxing match. Every time love is shown by any human being, it is a blow against the power of evil. Christians believe that Jesus' love, shown on Good Friday, was a knock-out blow. The opponent might stagger to his feet and carry on for a few more rounds, but it is only a matter of time before he falls.

Another way that Christians picture Good Friday is to imagine a war, as in the drama we have just seen. Wars are a series of battles. Sometimes there is a decisive battle and the turning point of the war is reached. There will be other battles, but the outcome is sure. Christians believe that Good Friday was the turning point in the war against wrong. People still experience evil, but Christians believe that the victory of God and good is certain. They believe we are living in that time between the decisive battle and the final surrender.

Something to think about

Look at the painting. Jesus is battle-scarred and he carries a flag which is the sign of victory in battle. Life can be a battle for all of us and sometimes we can feel defeated by it. This painting is a reminder that love can be a powerful weapon.

Optional prayer

In the battle of life, teach us, Lord, to use the weapons available to us – the weapons of love and hope, truth and faithfulness.

Music suggestions

'Now the green blade rises', *The Complete Come and Praise*, compiled by G. Marshall-Taylor (BBC, 1990).
'Christ triumphant', *Junior Praise 1*, compiled by P. Horrobin and G. Leavers (Marshall Pickering, 1986).

The Virgin and Child Enthroned (detail)

by Margarito of Arezzo

Background to the painting

Date: 1260s

Medium: tempera on wood

Dimensions: including frame 92.5 cm x 183 cm

This painting by Margarito of Arezzo *(Margar-eeto of Ahr-ettzo)* is the earliest Italian painting in the National Gallery. It is painted in the medieval Greek style (Byzantine). This detail is part of a larger painting, the full title of which is: **The Virgin and Child Enthroned, with Scenes of the Nativity and the Lives of the Saints.** The Virgin wears a crown and is seated on a lion-headed throne. The angels swing incense on either side – a symbol of worship. The Virgin Mary and Jesus are inside a mandorla (an almond shape): this is often used to indicate special status. The symbols of the evangelists (Matthew, Mark, Luke and John) are in the four corners and there are, in addition, eight scenes of the saints (not shown here). This painting was probably an altarpiece, possibly in a church dedicated to St John or St Nicholas as these saints occur in the part of the painting not included here.

Biblical material

Hebrews 4:14–16

We have someone who has gone before us and dwells with God in Heaven, Jesus, the Son of God. He has sympathy with us and understands our every weakness. He knows what we face because he too was tempted, but he did no wrong. So, when we need help, we should pray to God with confidence, knowing we will be treated with undeserved kindness and there we will always find help.

Luke 4:16–21

Jesus returned to his home town of Nazareth, the town where he had grown up. As usual he went to the synagogue, the place of worship, on the Sabbath day. He stood up to read and was given the book of the prophet Isaiah. He unrolled the scroll and read,

'The spirit of God is with me.
God has chosen me to tell good news to the poor.
He has sent me to announce freedom for those in
  prison,

to give sight to the blind,
to free people who suffer,
and to announce that the time has come for God
  to save his people.'

Jesus rolled up the scroll and gave it back to the man in charge and then he sat down. Everyone stared at him. Then Jesus said, 'What you have just heard me read has come true.'

Assembly 23

Themes: Good news/Gospel

Painting: The Virgin and Child Enthroned (detail)
by Margarito of Arezzo

You will need:
- Two tennis balls or a skipping rope
- Enlarged photograph of yourself (optional)
- Enlarged symbols of Gospel writers [O S23]
- CD player and recording of news bulletin (optional)
- Image of **The Virgin and Child Enthroned** [O P23/24]

Introduction

Younger pupils
In the days before television and computers, there were many traditional games, such as skipping, hopscotch and various ball games. Many of these games were accompanied by rhymes. Some of the rhymes came from the Bible. *Pupils might like to demonstrate traditional games, such as skipping, juggling two balls or bouncing a ball while saying the following rhyme:*

Matthew, Mark,
Luke and John,
Bless the bed
that I lie on.

This old rhyme provides the clue to understanding the painting.

Older pupils
Show some modern games or talk about them. Reminisce about traditional games which people played before the advent of computers and television. Quote the rhyme above and ask who Matthew, Mark, Luke and John were. Alternatively, demonstrate juggling with two balls while saying the rhyme.

Alternative
Talk about what sorts of things are good news, or read a piece of good news followed by bad news. Example: The good news is you have a day off on Friday. The bad news is we are setting you extra work to do at home.

Core material

Show the pupils a photograph of yourself. Ask how good a likeness it is.

When photography was first invented, some people thought that painting would die out. Why paint a picture when you can get a better likeness with a camera? This attitude assumed that paintings were all about copying, trying to make the painting look as near to real life as possible. Most paintings are not like that: they do more than copy reality. *Show the painting.* This painting by Margarito of Arezzo does not try to look 'real' at all. Look at Mary and the baby. Neither looks very 'real'. This artist was more concerned with communicating a message than trying to make things look real. But what is the message? The answer lies in the pictures in the four corners.

Matthew, Mark, Luke and John *(refer back to the rhyme in the introduction)* each wrote about Jesus. The books they wrote are called 'Gospels' which just means 'good news'. In the four corners of this painting are the symbols (signs) of the Gospel writers. Here is a drawing of these symbols. *Show the four symbols.* The sign for Matthew is a winged man. The sign for Mark is a winged lion. The sign for Luke is a winged ox and the sign for John is a rising eagle.

In the painting, Jesus holds a scroll in his right hand. It is a scroll of the good news. The message of this painting is about that good news which Jesus himself described when he first started teaching. *Read Luke 4:16–21.* Jesus taught the good news about the love and peace of God and God's forgiveness. That is why books about him are called gospels, meaning 'good news'.

Something to think about

If possible, play a recording of the opening of a news bulletin. If you could change one item of bad news into good news, what would it be? There are times when we feel that life gets on top of us, when all we hear is bad news. The time to get worried is when we hear largely good news on the television and in the newspapers. It is the unusual events that reach the news. All the time bad things feature on the news, it is a sign that love and peace are not rare.

Optional prayer

Thank you, God, for the good news that goes unreported every day. The stories of love, care and peace. Thank you, God, for the good news which Jesus brought, of your love, care and peace.

Music suggestions

'Go tell it on the mountain', *The Complete Come and Praise,* compiled by G. Marshall-Taylor (BBC, 1990).
'He came down', *Big Blue Planet,* edited by J. Jarvis (Stainer & Bell and Methodist Church Division of Education and Youth, 1995).

Assembly 24

Themes: Empathy/Son of Man, Son of God

Painting: The Virgin and Child Enthroned (detail)
by Margarito of Arezzo

You will need:
- A piano, keyboard, chime-bars or guitar
- Enlarged hybrid animals [✪ S24] (younger pupils)
- Magazine pictures and scissors (older pupils)
- Image of **The Virgin and Child Enthroned** [✪ P23/24]

Introduction

Younger pupils
Talk about books where you have pictures of the legs of one animal and the body of another. Use the illustrations provided to demonstrate these animals. Pupils can invent suitable names for them.

Older pupils
Show magazine pictures of people. Cut them in half and reassemble them so that the top half of one person is joined to the bottom half of another. Some pupils may like to do this before the assembly and show their hybrid people.

Core material

Show the painting. In this painting by Margarito of Arezzo, Jesus sits on his mother's lap. Although he is small, he does not look like a baby. He seems a strange mixture of child and adult.

Let's look at Jesus the baby:
He is baby-sized.
He sits on Mary's lap.

This is a reminder of the Christian belief that he is Mary's son and was born as a human baby in Bethlehem.

Now let's look at Jesus the adult:
He wears adult clothes.
He carries a scroll.
He raises a hand in blessing.
With Mary, Jesus is seated on a throne.

In this painting, Jesus wears the sort of clothes worn by important people of the time and carries a scroll. It is almost like painting a picture of a baby wearing a suit and carrying a briefcase. Babies do not play with scrolls. They wave their

arms about, they do not raise them in blessing. The throne is a symbol of kingship. 'King' is a title Christians use of God. Around Jesus is an almond shape, which often symbolizes heaven or God.

Why has the artist painted Jesus in such an unusual way? This curious mixture of baby and adult is the artist's way of expressing the Christian belief that Jesus was God's Son. He may have been born as a baby but he was important, so the artist gives him all the trappings of an important adult of the time.

Christians do not believe that Jesus was a 'half-and-half' person like the funny characters in picture books which have the body of one person and the legs of another. He was not half-God and half-man. Christians believe that God and man combined in Jesus. It is like two notes struck at the same time. *Ask pupils to demonstrate chords on the keyboard, piano or chime-bars. Older pupils might like to play chords on the guitar.*

Christians believe that Jesus was God's Son but they believe he lived as a human being and experienced what we experience. He worked as a carpenter and knew what it was to be tired. He had friends and enemies. He knew hunger and pain, love and laughter. Sometimes it is easier to talk to people who have been through an experience similar to the one you are experiencing. They know what you are going through. Christians believe that Jesus understands when people pray to him. He knows what life is like. *Read Hebrews 4:14–16.*

Something to think about

Think about people with whom you would share your problems and joys. Does it help if they have had similar experiences to the ones you are going through?

Optional prayer

Jesus, who walked in our shoes,
Help us on our way.
Jesus, who felt what we feel,
Comfort our hearts.
Jesus, who faced temptation,
Understand our temptations.

Music suggestions

'He came down', *Big Blue Planet,* edited by J. Jarvis (Stainer & Bell and Methodist Church Division of Education and Youth, 1995).
'Come and praise the Lord our King', *The Complete Come and Praise,* compiled by G. Marshall-Taylor (BBC, 1990).

Poems

for Assemblies 10 and 19

The Apostles' Rap by Colin Humphreys

Listen everybody to the things that I say,
As we name all the apostles in a special way.
There are twelve of these disciples in the following lines;
The followers of Jesus in Bible times.
There was Peter, Andrew, James and John,
Philip and Bartholomew and then Simon,
Thomas, Matthew and a second James,
Thaddaeus and Judas were the other names.
And now you know the names through this special rhyme,
Let's go through them one more time;
There was Peter, Andrew, James and John,
Philip and Bartholomew and then Simon,
Thomas, Matthew and a second James,
Thaddaeus and Judas were the other names.

Extract from 'The Whether Outlook' by Gordon Bailey

Whether I'm helpful when people despair,
Depends very largely on whether I care.
Whether I think that oppression's a crime,
Depends very largely on whether I've time.
Whether I go where my help is required,
Depends very largely on whether I'm tired.
Whether I'm generous, whether I'm mean,
Depends very largely on whether I'm keen.
Whether I honour the vows that I take,
Depends very largely on what I can make.
Whether I help someone burdened by care,
Depends very largely on whether I'm there.
Whether I love or I hope or I trust,
Depends very largely on whether I must.
Whether I comfort a friend who's afraid,
Depends very largely on whether I'm paid.

CD Index

The CD contains:
- **Images of the paintings** (prefix P) – These may be printed onto acetate for use on an overhead projector by the purchaser or the purchaser's school/organization only.
- **Resource sheets** (prefix S) – These provide additional material needed to deliver the assemblies or optional items such as drama scripts. All resource sheets may be printed, and enlarged on the photocopier if required.
- **PowerPoint slides** – For projecting paintings and material from resource sheets directly from the CD.

PAINTINGS AND RESOURCE SHEETS

Assembly 1

P1/2	*A Jesse Tree* attributed to Girolamo Genga
S1a	Identity Card – number only
S1b	Identity Card – number and name only
S1c	Identity Card – name, number and photograph
S1d	Family Tree

Assembly 2

P1/2	*A Jesse Tree* attributed to Girolamo Genga
S2a	Family Tree
S2b	Family Tree Information

Assembly 3

P3/4	*The Annunciation* by Duccio
S3a,b	Letters

Assembly 4

P3/4	*The Annunciation* by Duccio

Assembly 5

P5/6	*The Adoration of the Shepherds* by Guido Reni

Assembly 6

P5/6	*The Adoration of the Shepherds* by Guido Reni
S6	Christmas Action List

Assembly 7

P7/8	*The Marriage at Cana* by Mattia Preti
S7	The Waiter

Assembly 8

P7/8	*The Marriage at Cana* by Mattia Preti

Assembly 9

P9/10	*Christ teaching from Saint Peter's Boat on the Lake of Gennesaret* by Herman Saftleven
S9a,b	The Workers in the Vineyard
S9c,d	The Great Feast

Assembly 10

P9/10	*Christ teaching from Saint Peter's Boat on the Lake of Gennesaret* by Herman Saftleven

Assembly 11

P11/12	*Christ addressing a Kneeling Woman* by Paolo Veronese
S11	Outline of Person

Assembly 12

P11/12	*Christ addressing a Kneeling Woman* by Paolo Veronese
S12a	Frankenstein's Monster
S12b	Body Chemicals

Assembly 13

P13/14	*Christ blessing the Children* by Nicolaes Maes
S13	The Rights of the Child

Assembly 14

P13/14	*Christ blessing the Children* by Nicolaes Maes
S14	Important Moments

CD Index

Assembly 15

P15/16 *Christ washing his Disciples' Feet* by Jacopo Tintoretto
S15a Jobs and Powers
S15b Responsibilities

Assembly 16

P15/16 *Christ washing his Disciples' Feet* by Jacopo Tintoretto

Assembly 17

P17/18 *The Betrayal of Christ* by Ugolino di Nerio
S17a Relationships Web
S17b Jesus and His Friends Web

Assembly 18

P17/18 *The Betrayal of Christ* by Ugolino di Nerio
S18a Word-pictures
S18b Cup

Assembly 19

P19/20 *Christ carrying his Cross* by Giampietrino
S19 Outline of Person

Assembly 20

P19/20 *Christ carrying his Cross* by Giampietrino
S20a Cross
S20b Heart

Assembly 21

P21/22 *Christ rising from the Tomb* by Ferrari Gaudenzio
S21 Drama Outlines

Assembly 22

P21/22 *Christ rising from the Tomb* by Ferrari Gaudenzio
S22a Flag
S22b The Victory

Assembly 23

P23/24 *Virgin and Child Enthroned* (detail) by Margarito of Arezzo
S23 Symbols of Gospel Writers

Assembly 24

P23/24 *Virgin and Child Enthroned* (detail) by Margarito of Arezzo
S24 Hybrid Animals

POWERPOINT SLIDES

Sequences of more than one slide follow the order in which these slides should be shown in the assembly.

Assembly 1

S1a Identity Card – number only
S1b Identity Card – number and name only
S1c Identity Card – name, number and photograph
P1/2 *A Jesse Tree* attributed to Girolamo Genga
S1d Family Tree

Assembly 2

S2a Family Tree
P1/2 *A Jesse Tree* attributed to Girolamo Genga

Assemblies 3 and 4

P3/4 *The Annunciation* by Duccio

Assembly 5

P5/6 *The Adoration of the Shepherds* by Guido Reni

Assembly 6

S6 Christmas Action List
P5/6 *The Adoration of the Shepherds* by Guido Reni

Assemblies 7 and 8

P7/8 *The Marriage at Cana* by Mattia Preti

Assemblies 9 and 10

P9/10 *Christ teaching from Saint Peter's Boat on the Lake of Gennesaret* by Herman Saftleven

Assembly 11

S11 Outline of Person
P11/12 *Christ addressing a Kneeling Woman* by Paolo Veronese

CD Index

POWERPOINT SLIDES (continued)

Assembly 12

S12a   Frankenstein's Monster
S12b   Body Chemicals
P11/12 *Christ addressing a Kneeling Woman* by Paolo Veronese

Assembly 13

P13/14 *Christ blessing the Children* by Nicolaes Maes
S13   The Rights of the Child

Assembly 14

S14   Important Moments
P13/14 *Christ blessing the Children* by Nicolaes Maes

Assemblies 15 and 16

P15/16 *Christ washing his Disciples' Feet* by Jacopo Tintoretto

Assembly 17

S17a   Relationships Web
P17/18 *The Betrayal of Christ* by Ugolino di Nerio
S17b   Jesus and His Friends Web

Assembly 18

S18a   Word-pictures
P17/18 *The Betrayal of Christ* by Ugolino di Nerio
S18b   Cup

Assemblies 19 and 20

S19   Outline of Person (Assembly 19 only)
P19/20 *Christ carrying his Cross* by Giampietrino

Assembly 21

P21/22 *Christ rising from the Tomb* by Ferrari Gaudenzio

Assembly 22

S22a   Flag
P21/22 *Christ rising from the Tomb* by Ferrari Gaudenzio

Assembly 23

P23/24 *Virgin and Child Enthroned* (detail) by Margarito of Arezzo
S23   Symbols of Gospel Writers

Assembly 24

S24   Hybrid Animals
P23/24 *Virgin and Child Enthroned* (detail) by Margarito of Arezzo